time to cook
low carb
in 10, 20 & 30 minutes

p

This is a Parragon Book
First published in 2005

Parragon
Queen Street House
4 Queen Street
Bath BA1 1HE, UK

ISBN: 1-40544-992-6

Printed in Indonesia

Produced by the Bridgewater Book Company Ltd.

Note
This book uses metric and imperial measurements. Follow the same units of measurement throughout; do not mix metric and imperial. All spoon measurements are level: teaspoons are assumed to be 5 ml, and tablespoons are assumed to be 15 ml. Unless otherwise stated, milk is assumed to be full fat, eggs and individual vegetables such as potatoes are medium, and pepper is freshly ground black pepper.

The nutritional information provided for each recipe is per serving or per person. Optional ingredients, variations or serving suggestions have not been included in the calculations. The times given for each recipe are an approximate guide only, because the preparation times may differ according to the techniques used by different people and the cooking times may vary as a result of the type of oven used.

Recipes using raw or very lightly cooked eggs should be avoided by infants, the elderly, pregnant women, convalescents, and anyone suffering from an illness. Pregnant and breastfeeding women are advised to avoid eating peanuts and peanut products.

Key to symbols used in this book

 Preparation time

 Cooking time

 Serving number

Contents

Introduction

What constitutes a healthy diet? In one way, the answer to this question is very straightforward, while in another, it is almost impossible. It is true that a balanced intake of all the various food groups – carbohydrates, proteins and fats – in their appropriate proportions is the ideal that nutritionists encourage us to aim for. However, this raises a number of questions: where we are starting from, how old we are, what kind of lives we lead, whether we are men or women and even how to estimate a 'balanced intake' and 'appropriate proportions'. For various reasons, many of us have allowed the extra weight to creep on and have developed eating patterns that do our bodies no favours. A low-carb diet is one very successful way of tackling these sorts of problems.

WHAT ARE CARBOHYDRATES?
The name of this food group derives from the chemical elements it contains – carbon, hydrogen and oxygen – which form compounds such as starch and sugars. When these are eaten, the body breaks them down to release energy. They are found in a wide variety of foods, including grains, cereals, potatoes, some pulses such as peas and beans, and many popular snacks. Carbohydrates are comfort foods, making us feel full and satisfied.

There is a second type of carbohydrate that our bodies cannot digest and this is usually called dietary fibre. It contributes to the feeling of fullness after a meal and helps to regulate the digestive system, but the body cannot break it down to release energy. It is found in wheat bran, fruit, pulses, nuts and leafy green vegetables.

ENERGY AND BODY WEIGHT
The body needs energy to function. It obtains this from the food consumed, and the amount of energy you require depends on a number of factors. It is obvious that an athlete requires more input than an office worker, but age is also a consideration because the metabolism begins to slow down from about the age of 30. Body type also affects energy requirements. Energy is measured as calories. Many of the calories consumed are used quite quickly for everyday activities. The energy that

is not used is converted by the body to be stored in the muscles or as fat – if you consume more calories than you use, you will build up a store of fat.

The following is a guide to the approximate daily calories at different stages in life:

Boys and girls – 1800–2220 calories per day

Adults who exercise/have physical jobs
Men – 2850 calories per day
Women – 2150 calories per day

Adults who do not exercise/have sedentary jobs
Men – 2400 calories per day
Women – 2000 calories per day

Over 50s
Men – 2200 calories per day
Women – 1850 calories per day

HOW A LOW-CARB DIET CAN HELP

Carbohydrates are the main source of energy in our diets, with fats the second most important, so if you want to lose weight, reducing the intake of carbohydrates is a good way to do it. However, cutting them out altogether is neither sensible nor practical, because you will also be cutting out important nutrients. It is also unwise to embark on a drastic reduction of carbohydrates all at once. If you introduce this new eating pattern gradually, you will not encounter the mood swings or hunger pangs that so often go with attempts to diet and usually result in failure.

While it is true that taking in more energy than is expended is the reason why fat accumulates in the body, individual metabolism also plays a part and some people are simply more intolerant to carbohydrates than others. Pay attention to your body and respond to its particular needs.

For many, a low-carb diet is a lifetime choice, used to maintain their optimum weight, while others find it a quick way to shed a few pounds before a holiday. The choice is personal, but do remember that if you return to higher-carbohydrate meals, you are likely to regain weight.

Previously, the most difficult aspect of a low-carb diet was deciding what to eat, not what to leave out. The problem is now solved because this book provides a wealth of recipes for delicious, low-carb dishes, making it the perfect companion to whatever low-carb diet you choose to follow. There are even some tempting desserts that are lower in carbohydrates than most, making them ideal for occasional treats.

10 minutes to cook

All the planning and calorie-counting has been
done for you, so all you need to do to create
delicious, low-carbohydrate meals in 10 minutes for
your friends and family to enjoy is to organize your
ingredients and equipment before you begin.

10

8 mins

0 mins

serves 4

10 MINUTES TO COOK Guacamole

Serve this ever-popular Mexican avocado dip with a range of vegetable crudités. A spoonful of guacamole placed on plain grilled steak also makes a wonderful garnish.

Nutritional Information
Calories 245
Protein 3g
Carbohydrate 3g
Sugars 1g
Fat 25g
Saturates 6g

INGREDIENTS

3 avocados

2 tbsp lime juice

1 tbsp soured cream

1 tbsp olive oil

½ tsp cayenne pepper

3 spring onions, finely chopped

2 garlic cloves, finely chopped

salt

crudités, to serve

1 Cut the avocados in half lengthways and remove the stone, then scoop the flesh into a bowl. Add the lime juice and mash roughly with a fork.

2 Add the soured cream, olive oil, cayenne pepper, spring onions and garlic and season to taste with salt. Mash until well blended, but do not make the mixture completely smooth.

3 Transfer the guacamole to a serving bowl and serve immediately with crudités.

COOK'S TIP
If you are not using the guacamole immediately, cover tightly with clingfilm and leave to chill in the refrigerator for up to 2 hours.

8

10 MINUTES TO COOK   Taramasalata

This dip is excellent served with a selection of crudités, such as cucumber and carrot batons, pepper strips and celery sticks.

Nutritional Information
Calories 130
Protein 6g
Carbohydrate 7g
Sugars 1g
Fat 9g
Saturates 1g

INGREDIENTS

55 g/2 oz white bread

milk, to soak

1 garlic clove

75 g/2¾ oz smoked cod's roe

pinch of cayenne pepper

3–6 tbsp lemon juice

2–4 tbsp sunflower oil

TO GARNISH

cracked pepper

lemon slice quarter

sprig of fresh flat-leaf parsley

TO SERVE

shredded fresh green salad leaves

crudités

1 Remove the crusts from the bread and soak in the milk for 5 minutes, or until soft. Squeeze dry, reserving the liquid.

2 Crush the garlic, place in a food processor with the cod's roe, bread and cayenne pepper and blend until smooth. Slowly add the lemon juice and sunflower oil, tasting frequently. Add the milk that was used to soak the bread if the consistency is not quite smooth enough.

3 Transfer the taramasalata to a serving dish, garnish with a sprig of fresh flat-leaf parsley and serve with fresh green salad leaves and crudités.

COOK'S TIP
If not using immediately, cover with clingfilm and leave to chill in the refrigerator until 30 minutes before you need it.

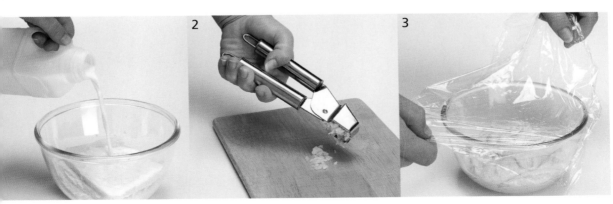

10 MINUTES TO COOK Vegetable Cream Dip

Instead of raw crudités, try a selection of lightly cooked baby vegetables, such as corn cobs, mangetout and carrots to serve with this dip.

Nutritional Information
Calories 266
Protein 4g
Carbohydrate 3g
Sugars 3g
Fat 27g
Saturates 17g

INGREDIENTS

225 g/8 oz cream cheese
125 ml/4 fl oz natural yogurt or soured cream
1 tbsp fresh parsley, finely chopped
1 tbsp fresh thyme, finely chopped
2 spring onions, finely chopped
shredded spring onion, to garnish

1 Beat the cream cheese in a large bowl until soft and smooth.

2 Add the yogurt, chopped herbs and 1 spring onion and mix well.

3 Transfer to a serving dish and sprinkle the remaining finely chopped spring onion over the top. Garnish with the shredded spring onion and serve.

COOK'S TIP
If you have time, this dip tastes even better if it is chilled. Cover the mixture with clingfilm and leave to chill in the refrigerator for at least 30 minutes. Stir thoroughly before transferring to a serving dish.

10 MINUTES TO COOK   Two Classic Salsas

*A Mexican meal is not complete
without an accompanying salsa.
These two salsas are ideal for
seasoning any traditional dish.*

Nutritional Information
Calories 21
Protein 1g
Carbohydrate 4g
Sugars 3g
Fat 0g
Saturates 0g

INGREDIENTS

JALAPEÑO SALSA

1 onion, finely chopped

2–3 garlic cloves, finely chopped

4–6 tbsp roughly chopped pickled
    jalapeño chillies

juice of ½ lemon

about ¼ tsp ground cumin

salt

SALSA CRUDA

6–8 ripe tomatoes, finely chopped

about 100 ml/3½ fl oz tomato juice

3–4 garlic cloves, finely chopped

½–1 bunch of fresh coriander leaves,
    roughly chopped

pinch of sugar

3–4 fresh green chillies, such as jalapeño or
    serrano, deseeded and finely chopped

½–1 tsp ground cumin

3–4 spring onions, finely chopped

salt

whole chillies, to garnish

1 To make the Jalapeño Salsa, place
the onion in a bowl with the garlic,
jalapeños, lemon juice and cumin.
Season to taste with salt and stir
together. Cover with clingfilm and
chill in the refrigerator until required.

2 To make a chunky-textured Salsa
Cruda, stir all the ingredients together
in a bowl and season to taste with salt.
Cover with clingfilm and chill in the
refrigerator until required.

3 To make a smoother-textured salsa,
process the ingredients in a food
processor. Scrape into a bowl, cover
and chill as above. Garnish the salsas
with whole chillies and serve as an
accompaniment or a dip.

COOK'S TIP
You can vary the amount of garlic,
chillies and ground spices according
to taste, but make sure the salsas
have quite a 'kick', otherwise they
will not be effective.

10 MINUTES TO COOK Prawn Cocktail

This classic starter will impress your guests whatever the occasion. If using frozen prawns, make sure they are completely thawed before you begin.

Nutritional Information

Calories 667
Protein 14g
Carbohydrate 8g
Sugars 8g
Fat 65g
Saturates 9g

INGREDIENTS

1 avocado

1 tbsp lemon juice

500 g/1 lb 2 oz cooked peeled prawns, thawed if frozen

fresh green lettuce leaves

DRESSING

1 egg

2 tsp sherry vinegar

½ tsp mustard

dash of Worcestershire sauce

pinch of salt

300 ml/10 fl oz sunflower oil

100 ml/3½ fl oz tomato ketchup

TO GARNISH

pinch of paprika

strips of lemon zest

4 whole cooked prawns (optional)

1 To make the dressing, break the egg into a food processor. Add the vinegar, mustard, Worcestershire sauce and salt and process for 15 seconds. While the motor is still running, slowly pour the sunflower oil through the feeder tube until thoroughly incorporated. Transfer the dressing to a large bowl, then stir in the tomato ketchup. Cover with clingfilm and leave to chill in the refrigerator until required.

2 Cut the avocado in half lengthways, then remove and discard the stone and skin. Cut the flesh into slices, then brush the slices with lemon juice to prevent discoloration.

3 To assemble the salad, take the dressing from the refrigerator, add the avocado and prawns and stir gently until coated.

4 Divide the lettuce leaves between large individual serving glasses or bowls. Fill each one with prawns, then garnish with paprika and lemon zest strips. If using whole prawns, hang a whole cooked prawn on the rim of each glass or bowl. Serve immediately.

10 MINUTES TO COOK Chicory Salad

The contrast of the pink grapefruit, creamy chicory and bright green lamb's lettuce makes this dish look simply stunning.

Nutritional Information
Calories 137
Protein 1g
Carbohydrate 4g
Sugars 4g
Fat 13g
Saturates 2g

INGREDIENTS

1 pink grapefruit

1 avocado

55 g/2 oz lamb's lettuce

2 heads of chicory, diagonally sliced

1 bunch of fresh mint, chopped, plus extra
   sprigs to garnish (optional)

FRENCH DRESSING

3 tbsp olive oil

1 tbsp wine vinegar

1 small garlic clove, crushed

½ tsp Dijon or Meaux mustard

1 tsp clear honey

salt and pepper

1 Peel the grapefruit with a serrated knife. Cut the grapefruit into segments by cutting between the membranes. Reserve until required.

2 To make the French dressing, place the olive oil, vinegar, garlic, mustard and honey in a screw-top jar and shake well to mix. Season to taste with salt and pepper, then pour into a bowl.

3 Cut the avocado in half lengthways, then remove and discard the stone and skin. Cut the flesh into thin slices, then place in the bowl of dressing and toss gently until coated.

4 Remove any stalks from the lamb's lettuce and place in a bowl with the grapefruit, chicory and chopped mint.

5 Add the avocado and 2 tablespoons of the dressing. Toss well and transfer to serving plates. Serve immediately.

COOK'S TIP
Lamb's lettuce is so called because the shape of its dark green leaves resembles a lamb's tongue. It is also known as corn salad and the French call it mâche. It is easy to grow in the garden and will withstand frost.

18

1

3

10 MINUTES TO COOK Anchovy & Olive Salad

To save time, buy olives that are already stoned, but if they are stored in brine, make sure that they are rinsed thoroughly before using.

Nutritional Information
Calories 152
Protein 2g
Carbohydrate 2g
Sugars 2g
Fat 15g
Saturates 2g

INGREDIENTS

large handful mixed lettuce leaves
20 black olives
12 cherry tomatoes
1 tbsp chopped fresh oregano
6 canned anchovy fillets, drained
DRESSING
4 tbsp extra virgin olive oil
1 tbsp white wine vinegar
1 tbsp lemon juice
1 tbsp chopped fresh flat-leaf parsley
salt and pepper
lemon wedges, to garnish

1 To make the dressing, place all the ingredients in a small bowl, season to taste with salt and pepper and stir together well.

2 To assemble the salad, arrange the lettuce leaves in a serving dish. Stone and halve the olives, halve the cherry tomatoes, then scatter the olives and tomatoes on top of the lettuce leaves with the oregano. Thinly slice the anchovies and add to the salad. Drizzle over the dressing. Serve on individual plates garnished with lemon wedges.

10 MINUTES
TO COOK

Spicy Chicken Salad

This is an excellent recipe for leftover roast chicken. Add the dressing just before serving, so that the spinach retains its crispness.

Nutritional Information
Calories 225
Protein 25g
Carbohydrate 4g
Sugars 4g
Fat 12g
Saturates 2g

INGREDIENTS

225 g/8 oz young spinach leaves

3 celery sticks, thinly sliced

½ cucumber, thinly sliced

2 spring onions, thinly sliced

3 tbsp chopped fresh parsley

350 g/12 oz boneless, lean roast chicken, thinly sliced

smoked almonds, to garnish (optional)

DRESSING

2.5-cm/1-inch piece fresh root ginger, finely grated

3 tbsp olive oil

1 tbsp white wine vinegar

1 tbsp clear honey

½ tsp ground cinnamon

salt and pepper

1 Thoroughly wash the spinach leaves and pat dry on kitchen paper.

2 Place the spinach in a large bowl, then add the celery, cucumber, spring onions and parsley and toss well.

3 Transfer the salad ingredients to serving plates and arrange the chicken on top.

4 To make the dressing, place the grated ginger, olive oil, vinegar, honey and cinnamon in a screw-top jar and shake well to mix. Season to taste with salt and pepper.

5 Pour the dressing over the salad. Scatter a few smoked almonds over the salad to garnish, if using.

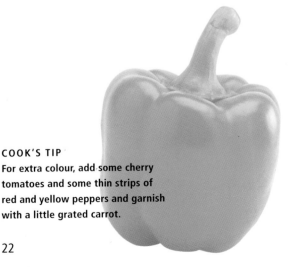

COOK'S TIP
For extra colour, add some cherry tomatoes and some thin strips of red and yellow peppers and garnish with a little grated carrot.

Beetroot, Apple & Celery Salad

Try to buy cooked beetroot that is not stored in vinegar because this may spoil the flavour of the finished dish.

Nutritional Information
Calories 55
Protein 2g
Carbohydrate 11g
Sugars 11g
Fat <1g
Saturates <1g

INGREDIENTS

2 apples
2 large or 4 small cooked beetroot
2 celery sticks
100 ml/3½ fl oz natural yogurt
1 tbsp lemon juice

1 Wash and core the apples, but leave the skin on. Grate them into a large salad bowl.

2 Grate the beetroot, then add it to the bowl with the apples. Wash and trim the celery sticks, cut them into small pieces, then add them to the salad bowl.

3 Add the yogurt and lemon juice, mix until all the ingredients are thoroughly combined, then serve.

10 MINUTES
TO COOK

Greek Feta Salad

This classic salad is a great summer lunch dish. If you cannot find vine leaves, then use salad leaves instead.

Nutritional Information

Calories 186
Protein 6g
Carbohydrate 7g
Sugars 6g
Fat 15g
Saturates 5g

INGREDIENTS

½ cucumber
115 g/4 oz feta cheese (drained weight)
few vine leaves
4 tomatoes, sliced
1 small red onion, thinly sliced
8 black olives
DRESSING
3 tbsp extra virgin olive oil
1 tbsp lemon juice
½ tsp dried oregano
salt and pepper

1 To make the dressing, place the olive oil, lemon juice and oregano into a jog, season to taste with salt and pepper and stir or shake well to mix.

2 Halve the cucumber lengthways, then peel and slice. Cut the feta into cubes. Arrange the vine leaves on a serving dish and then the tomatoes, cucumber and onion. Scatter the cheese and olives on top. Pour the dressing over the salad and serve.

10 MINUTES TO COOK Figs & Parma Ham

This colourful fresh salad is delicious at any time of the year. Prosciutto di Parma is thought to be the best ham in the world.

Nutritional Information
Calories 121
Protein 1g
Carbohydrate 6g
Sugars 6g
Fat 11g
Saturates 2g

INGREDIENTS

40 g/1½ oz rocket

4 fresh figs

4 slices Parma ham

4 tbsp olive oil

1 tbsp fresh orange juice

1 tbsp clear honey

1 small fresh red chilli

1 Tear the rocket into manageable pieces and arrange on 4 individual serving plates.

2 Using a sharp knife, cut each of the figs into quarters and place them on top of the rocket leaves.

3 Using a sharp knife, cut the Parma ham into strips and scatter over the rocket and figs.

4 Place the olive oil, orange juice and honey in a screw-top jar and shake well until the mixture emulsifies and forms a thick dressing. Transfer the dressing to a bowl.

5 Using a sharp knife, dice the chilli. (You can remove the seeds first if you prefer a milder flavour.) Add the chopped chilli to the dressing and mix well.

6 Drizzle the dressing over the Parma ham, rocket and figs, tossing to mix well. Serve immediately.

COOK'S TIP
Chillies can burn the skin for several hours after chopping, so it is advisable to wear gloves when you are handling any very hot varieties and to wash your hands thoroughly afterwards.

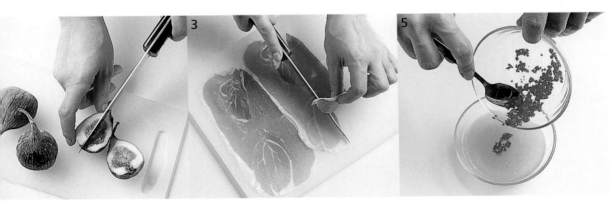

Celery with Olive Cheese Filling

These filled celery sticks are simple to prepare and make an ideal snack or lunch if you do not have a lot of time.

Nutritional Information
Calories 274
Protein 3g
Carbohydrate 2g
Sugars 2g
Fat 29g
Saturates 17g

INGREDIENTS

12 celery sticks

225 g/8 oz cream cheese

55 g/2 oz black or green olives, stoned and finely chopped

55 g/2 oz pimiento, finely chopped

2 spring onions, finely chopped

1 tbsp finely chopped fresh parsley

2 tsp Tabasco or hot pepper sauce (optional)

1 Trim the celery sticks, removing all the leaves and any rough strings.

2 Beat the cream cheese in a mixing bowl until soft and smooth. Add all the other ingredients and mix well.

3 Spoon or pipe the cream cheese into the celery sticks. Cut the sticks into 5-cm/2-inch pieces and arrange on an attractive serving dish.

10 MINUTES TO COOK

Prawn & Mango Salad

Mangoes and prawns are quite an unusual combination but they work extremely well in this delicious salad.

Nutritional Information
Calories 146
Protein 16g
Carbohydrate 15g
Sugars 14g
Fat 3g
Saturates 0.5g

INGREDIENTS

2 mangoes

225 g/8 oz cooked peeled prawns, thawed if frozen

mixed salad leaves

4 whole cooked prawns, to garnish

DRESSING

6 tbsp low-fat natural yogurt

2 tbsp reduced-calorie mayonnaise

1 tbsp lemon juice

salt and pepper

1 Cutting close to the stone, cut a large slice from 1 side of each mango, then cut another slice from the opposite side. Without breaking the skin, cut the flesh in the segments into squares, then push the skin inside out to expose the cubes and cut away from the skin. Use a sharp knife to peel the remaining centre section and cut the flesh away from the stone into cubes. Reserve any juice in a bowl and place the mango flesh in a separate bowl.

2 Add the prawns to the mango flesh. To the juice, add the yogurt, mayonnaise, lemon juice and salt and pepper to taste and blend together.

3 Arrange the salad leaves in a serving dish and add the mango flesh and prawns. Pour over the dressing and serve garnished with whole prawns.

10 MINUTES TO COOK

Green Sesame Salad

A very elegant and light salad, which will complement rice and noodle dishes beautifully.

Nutritional Information
Calories 78
Protein 3g
Carbohydrate 3g
Sugars 8g
Fat 3g
Saturates 0.5g

INGREDIENTS

125 g/4½ oz beansprouts

3 celery sticks

1 large green pepper, deseeded

1 large Granny Smith apple

2 tbsp toasted sesame seeds, to garnish

DRESSING

1½ tbsp chopped fresh coriander

3 tbsp fresh lime juice

½ tsp mild chilli powder

1 tsp sugar

½ tsp salt

1 Soak the beansprouts for 1 minute, then drain thoroughly.

2 Pick over the beansprouts, removing any that seem a little brown or limp – it is essential that they are fresh and crunchy for this recipe.

3 To make the dressing, place the coriander, lime juice, chilli powder, sugar and salt in a small bowl and mix thoroughly.

4 Using a sharp knife, cut the celery into 2.5-cm/1-inch pieces. Cut the pepper into small pieces and the Granny Smith apple into small chunks.

5 Place the celery, pepper and apple in the bowl containing the beansprouts and stir gently to mix.

6 Just before serving, pour the dressing over the salad, tossing well to mix.

7 Garnish the green sesame salad with the toasted sesame seeds and serve immediately.

COOK'S TIP
Keeping each ingredient as fresh and crunchy as possible will make all the difference to the appearance and taste of this elegant salad. To prevent the apples going brown, soak the slices briefly in a little lemon juice and water as soon as you have cut them.

3

5

Mixed Cabbage Coleslaw with Fruit

10 MINUTES TO COOK

Coleslaw is traditionally a favourite at parties and barbecues and this version is no exception. It is not only quick to make but is nutritious as well.

2 Mix the mayonnaise and lemon juice together in a separate bowl. Season to taste with salt and pepper and pour over the salad. Mix all the ingredients together until well combined, then serve immediately.

Nutritional Information
Calories 249
Protein 2g
Carbohydrate 18g
Sugars 17g
Fat 19g
Saturates 3g

INGREDIENTS

115 g/4 oz white cabbage
115 g/4 oz red cabbage
2 large carrots
1 large onion
25 g/1 oz sultanas
25 g/1 oz raisins
100 ml/3½ fl oz mayonnaise
2 tbsp lemon juice
salt and pepper

1 Wash and shred the white and red cabbage. Grate the carrots and finely chop the onion. Place all the prepared vegetables in a large salad bowl, then wash the sultanas and raisins and add them to the bowl.

COOK'S TIP
If not using immediately, cover with clingfilm and leave to chill in the refrigerator until ready to use.

10 MINUTES TO COOK **Tropical Salad**

Pawpaws are ready to eat when they yield to gentle pressure. Serve in the shells of baby pineapples for a stunning effect.

Nutritional Information
Calories 69
Protein 1g
Carbohydrate 14g
Sugars 13g
Fat 0.3g
Saturates 0g

INGREDIENTS

1 pawpaw

2 tbsp fresh orange juice

3 tbsp rum

2 bananas

2 guavas

1 small pineapple or 2 baby pineapples

2 passion fruit

pineapple leaves, to decorate

1 Cut the pawpaw in half and remove the seeds. Peel and slice the flesh into a bowl.

2 Pour over the orange juice together with the rum.

3 Peel and slice the bananas, then peel and slice the guavas, and add both to the bowl.

4 Cut the top and base from the pineapple, cut off the skin and flick out the 'eyes' with the point of a knife.

5 Slice the pineapple flesh, remove and discard the core, then cut into pieces and add to the bowl.

6 Halve the passion fruit, scoop out the flesh with a teaspoon, add to the bowl and stir well to mix.

7 Spoon the salad into glass bowls and decorate with pineapple leaves.

COOK'S TIP
Guavas have a heavenly smell when ripe – their scent will fill a whole room. They should give to gentle pressure when ripe, and their skins should be yellow. The canned varieties are very good and have a pink tinge to the flesh.

10 MINUTES TO COOK   Glazed Pineapple Slices

A very simple dessert to make when you are short of time. These pineapple slices are particularly delicious served with either a spoonful of vanilla ice cream or fruit sorbet.

Nutritional Information
Calories 313
Protein 1g
Carbohydrate 26g
Sugars 26g
Fat 24g
Saturates 16g

INGREDIENTS

1 pineapple
50 ml/2 fl oz honey
115 g/4 oz butter, melted
fresh mint sprigs, to decorate
SERVING SUGGESTIONS
fruit sorbet
crème fraîche
whipped cream
ice cream

1 Peel and core the pineapple. Cut into thick slices, about 2.5 cm/1 inch wide.

2 Preheat the griddle over a medium heat. Meanwhile, heat the honey in a small saucepan over a medium heat, or in the microwave, until it is liquid.

3 Brush both sides of the pineapple slices with the melted butter. Place on the griddle and cook for 2 minutes on each side, brushing with honey before and after turning so that both sides are well coated and sticky.

4 Remove the hot pineapple from the griddle and divide between serving plates. Decorate with mint sprigs and serve with a scoop of sorbet, crème fraîche, whipped cream or ice cream.

10 MINUTES TO COOK   **Rum Bananas**

These are a popular dessert, which you can serve whatever the occasion, from an impromtu supper party to a family gathering. It is best to choose ripe bananas for this recipe.

Nutritional Information
Calories 129
Protein 1g
Carbohydrate 24g
Sugars 22g
Fat <1g
Saturates <1g

INGREDIENTS

4 bananas

4 tsp rum or Cointreau

SERVING SUGGESTIONS

sorbet

ice cream

double cream

crème fraîche

1 Preheat the griddle over a high heat.

2 Place the bananas, still in their skins, on the griddle. Cook for 5–10 minutes, or until the skins are black, turning occasionally.

3 Remove the bananas from the griddle, peel and place in individual serving bowls. Pour 1 teaspoonful of rum over each banana and serve while still hot, with a scoop of sorbet, ice cream, double cream or crème fraîche.

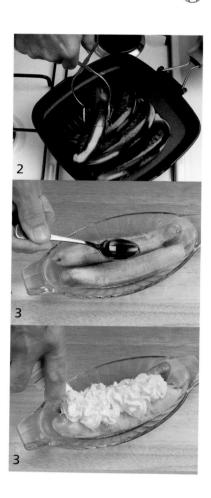

20 minutes to cook

you want a nutritious meal but don't want to spend
ong in the kitchen, there are plenty of recipes in
his section to choose from. Fluffy Prawn Omelettes
nd Spicy Tomato Chicken are just a couple of the
ishes that can be created in 20 minutes.

20

Fluffy Prawn Omelette

Having a rich protein source such as prawns for breakfast sets up the day for stable blood sugar and energy release.

Nutritional Information
Calories 157
Protein 12g
Carbohydrate 3.2g
Sugars 2.3g
Fat 11g
Saturates 3.5g

INGREDIENTS

115 g/4 oz thawed cooked peeled prawns
4 spring onions, chopped
55 g/2 oz courgette, grated
4 eggs, separated
few dashes of Tabasco sauce, to taste
3 tbsp milk
1 tbsp sunflower or olive oil
25 g/1 oz mature Cheddar cheese, grated
salt and pepper

1 Pat the prawns dry with kitchen paper, then mix with the spring onions and courgette in a bowl and reserve.

2 Using a fork, beat the egg yolks with the Tabasco sauce, milk and salt and pepper to taste in a separate bowl.

3 Whisk the egg whites in a large bowl until stiff, then gently stir the egg yolk mixture into the egg whites, taking care not to over-mix.

4 Heat the sunflower oil in a large, non-stick frying pan and, when hot, pour in the egg mixture. Cook over a low heat for 4–6 minutes, or until lightly set. Preheat the grill.

5 Spoon the prawn mixture on top of the eggs and sprinkle with the cheese. Cook under the hot grill for 2–3 minutes, or until set and the top is golden brown. Cut into wedges and serve immediately.

20 MINUTES TO COOK

Scrambled Eggs with Asparagus

serves 4

Asparagus is alkalizing, which means that it helps to clear the kidneys and is a good antidote for rich acidic foods such as meat and dairy.

Nutritional Information
Calories 255
Protein 16g
Carbohydrate 3.7g
Sugars 1.4g
Fat 20g
Saturates 10.4g

INGREDIENTS

55 g/2 oz unsalted butter

115 g/4 oz baby asparagus spears, diagonally sliced

85 g/3 oz button mushrooms, sliced

4 eggs

3 tbsp single cream

4 thick slices cooked lean ham

1–2 tbsp snipped fresh chives

salt and pepper

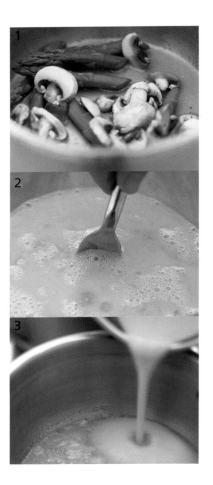

1 Melt half the butter in a frying pan over a medium heat, add the asparagus and mushrooms and cook, stirring frequently, for 5 minutes, or until softened. Remove from the frying pan, drain if necessary and keep warm.

2 Beat the eggs with the cream and salt and pepper to taste in a medium-sized bowl.

3 Melt the remaining butter in a non-stick saucepan over a medium heat. Pour in the egg mixture and cook, stirring gently with a wooden spoon, for 5–6 minutes, or until lightly set.

4 Arrange the ham on individual serving plates, top with the asparagus and mushrooms, then the egg scramble. Sprinkle with the chives and serve immediately.

20 MINUTES TO COOK

Piperade

Red and orange peppers contain beta-carotene, a powerful antioxidant that is found in red, yellow and orange vegetables and fruit.

Nutritional Information
Calories 268
Protein 15g
Carbohydrate 15g
Sugars 8.4g
Fat 17g
Saturates 3.2g

INGREDIENTS

1 onion, finely chopped

1 tbsp olive oil

1–2 garlic cloves (optional), crushed or chopped

1 red pepper, deseeded and cut into thin strips

1 orange pepper, deseeded and cut into thin strips

85 g/3 oz courgette, roughly grated

4 eggs

3 tbsp cold water

salt and pepper

1 tbsp chopped fresh basil

1 Finely chop the onion and reserve. Heat the oil in a non-stick frying pan over a medium heat, add the onion, garlic, if using, and peppers and cook, stirring frequently, for 5 minutes, or until softened. Stir in the courgette.

2 Beat the eggs with the water and salt and pepper to taste in a medium-sized bowl, then pour over the onion and pepper mixture. Using a fork or wooden spatula, gently draw the mixture from the edges of the pan into the centre, allowing the uncooked egg to flow to the edges of the frying pan.

3 When the egg is lightly set, sprinkle the top with the basil and cook for a further 1–2 minutes, or until cooked to your personal preference.

4 Cut into wedges and serve immediately.

Bacon & Tomato Scramble

Eggs contain lecithin, which helps break down fats in the liver, and sulphur, which helps clear out toxins and alcohol from the liver.

Nutritional Information

Calories 272
Protein 16g
Carbohydrate 6.9g
Sugars 4.6g
Fat 20.5g
Saturates 7.5g

INGREDIENTS

8 lean back bacon rashers

2 beef or 4 medium tomatoes, halved

4 eggs

3 tbsp milk

1 tbsp snipped fresh chives, plus extra to garnish (optional)

1 tbsp unsalted butter

salt and pepper

1 Preheat the grill to high and cover the grill rack with foil. Arrange the bacon on the foil and cook under the preheated grill for 3–4 minutes on each side, or until crisp. About 3 minutes before the end of cooking time, add the tomatoes, cut-side up, and cook for the remainder of the cooking time.

2 Meanwhile, beat the eggs, milk and salt and pepper to taste in a medium-sized bowl, then stir in the chives.

3 Melt the butter in a non-stick saucepan over a medium heat, pour in the egg mixture and cook, stirring gently with a wooden spoon, for 5–6 minutes, or until lightly set.

4 Arrange the egg scramble with the cooked bacon and tomatoes on warmed serving plates and serve immediately. Garnish with extra snipped chives, if you like.

Devilled Eggs

These filled eggs are perfect served as canapés or as part of a barbecue party. Make sure the anchovies are rinsed thoroughly before using.

Nutritional Information

Calories 185
Protein 16g
Carbohydrate 0g
Sugars 0g
Fat 13g
Saturates 3g

INGREDIENTS

8 hard-boiled eggs

2 tbsp canned tuna, drained

4 canned anchovy fillets, drained and rinsed

6 black olives, stoned

1 tsp capers

1 Peel the eggs, cut in half lengthways and remove the yolks. Mash the yolks, or place in a food processor together with the tuna, 2 anchovies, 4 olives and all of the capers.

2 Blend the ingredients together to make a smooth paste, adding 1 teaspoon of oil from the tuna or anchovies, or some extra virgin olive oil, to achieve the correct consistency.

3 Fill the egg white hollows with the yolk mixture using either a teaspoon or a piping bag. Make sure the filling is piled high. Arrange the egg whites on an attractive serving dish.

4 Garnish the filled eggs with the remaining anchovies and olives, cut into tiny strips, and serve.

Eight Jewel Vegetables

This recipe, as the title suggests, is a colourful mixture of eight vegetables, cooked in a black bean and soy sauce.

Nutritional Information

Calories 110
Protein 4g
Carbohydrate 7g
Sugars 3g
Fat 8g
Saturates 1g

INGREDIENTS

2 tbsp groundnut oil

6 spring onions, sliced

3 garlic cloves, crushed

1 green pepper, deseeded and diced

1 red pepper, deseeded and diced

1 fresh red chilli, deseeded and sliced

2 tbsp chopped water chestnuts

1 courgette, chopped

125 g/4½ oz oyster mushrooms

3 tbsp black bean sauce

2 tsp Chinese rice wine or dry sherry

4 tbsp dark soy sauce

1 tsp dark brown sugar

2 tbsp water

1 tsp sesame oil

1 Heat the groundnut oil in a preheated wok or large frying pan until it is almost smoking.

2 Reduce the heat slightly, add the spring onions and garlic and stir-fry for about 30 seconds.

3 Add the peppers, chilli, water chestnuts and courgette to the wok and stir-fry for 2–3 minutes, or until the vegetables are just beginning to soften.

4 Add the oyster mushrooms, black bean sauce, rice wine, soy sauce, sugar and water to the wok and stir-fry for an additional 4 minutes.

5 Sprinkle the stir-fry with sesame oil and serve immediately.

Grandma's Chopped Herring

This quick and easy dish is perfect served as a starter for an informal supper or as part of a summer lunch party.

Nutritional Information
Calories 248
Protein 19g
Carbohydrate 15g
Sugars 11g
Fat 13g
Saturates 1g

INGREDIENTS

4 rollmops, with onions
2 hard-boiled eggs
1 cooking apple
1 tbsp matzoh meal or fine breadcrumbs

1 Skin the rollmops and chop with the onions, eggs and apple.

2 Mix in the matzoh meal and turn into a serving dish.

COOK'S TIP
If not using immediately, cover with clingfilm and leave to chill in the refrigerator until 10 minutes before you need it.

20 MINUTES TO COOK

Chicken & Chipotle Soup

This soup evolved from the foodstalls that line the streets of Tlalpan, a suburb of Mexico City: avocado, chicken and chillies make it special.

Nutritional Information

Calories 216
Protein 28g
Carbohydrate 2g
Sugars 1g
Fat 11g
Saturates 2g

INGREDIENTS

1.5 litres/2¾ pints chicken stock

2–3 garlic cloves, finely chopped

1–2 chipotle chillies, cut into very thin strips (see Cook's Tip)

1 avocado

lime or lemon juice, for tossing

3–5 spring onions, thinly sliced

350–400 g/12–14 oz skinless, boneless cooked chicken breast, torn or cut into shreds or thin strips

2 tbsp chopped fresh coriander

1 lime, cut into wedges, to serve

1 Place the chicken stock in a saucepan with the garlic and chipotle chillies and bring to the boil.

2 Meanwhile, cut the avocado in half lengthways, then remove and discard the stone and skin. Dice the flesh and toss in lime juice to prevent the flesh turning brown.

3 Arrange the spring onions, chicken, avocado and fresh coriander in the base of 4 individual soup bowls or in a large tureen.

4 Ladle the hot stock into the bowls and serve with lime wedges.

COOK'S TIP
Chipotle chillies are smoked and dried jalapeño chillies and are available canned or dried. They add a distinctive smoky flavour to dishes and are very hot. Drain canned chipotles before using. Dried chipotle chillies need to be reconstituted before using.

60

Crudités with Garlic Chive & Coriander Dip

20 MINUTES TO COOK

Raw vegetables are the ideal healthy start to a meal, but creamy dips can undo all your good intentions. This is the perfect solution – all the richness and flavour, but none of the fat.

Nutritional Information
Calories 67
Protein 7g
Carbohydrate 9g
Sugars 8g
Fat 1g
Saturates 0g

INGREDIENTS

CRUDITÉS
115 g/4 oz baby corn cobs
115 g/4 oz young asparagus spears, trimmed
1 head of chicory, leaves separated
1 red pepper, deseeded and sliced
1 orange pepper, deseeded and sliced
8 radishes, trimmed
DIP
1 tbsp hot water
1 tsp saffron threads
225 g/8 oz fat-free fromage frais
3 tbsp chopped fresh coriander
1 tbsp snipped fresh garlic chives
salt and pepper
fresh coriander sprigs, to garnish (optional)

1 Blanch the corn and asparagus in separate saucepans of boiling water for 2 minutes. Drain, plunge into iced water and drain again. Arrange all the vegetables on a serving platter and cover with a damp tea towel.

2 To make the dip, place the hot water in a small bowl. Lightly crush the saffron threads between your fingers and add to the bowl, then leave to stand for 3–4 minutes, or until the water is a rich golden colour.

3 Place the fromage frais in a separate bowl and beat until smooth, then beat in the infused saffron water. Stir in the chopped coriander and snipped chives and season to taste with salt and pepper. Transfer to a serving bowl and garnish with a few sprigs of fresh coriander, if using. Serve immediately with the prepared vegetables.

COOK'S TIP
The fat content of fromage frais ranges between 0 and 8 per cent. This is reflected in the consistency. Fat-free fromage frais is excellent for dips because it is soft and easily mixed with other ingredients.

Scallops on Horseback

20 MINUTES TO COOK

These tasty little morsels would make wonderful hot canapés to serve at a dinner party with pre-dinner drinks.

Nutritional Information
Calories 485
Protein 53g
Carbohydrate 4g
Sugars 0g
Fat 29g
Saturates 10g

INGREDIENTS

20 thawed prepared scallops
2–3 tbsp lemon juice
20 rindless streaky bacon rashers
salt and pepper
tartare sauce, to serve

1 Preheat the grill to medium. Sprinkle the scallops with lemon juice and season to taste with salt and pepper.

2 Stretch the bacon with a flat-bladed knife, then wrap a rasher around each scallop, securing it with a wooden cocktail stick.

3 Cook under the hot grill for 5 minutes on each side, or until cooked through. Serve immediately with tartare sauce.

COOK'S TIP
To make a speedy tartare sauce, stir 2 tablespoons each of chopped gherkins and capers into 300 ml/10 fl oz ready-made mayonnaise. Stir in snipped chives or finely chopped spring onions to taste, then serve.

20 MINUTES TO COOK

Antipasto Volente

In Italy, antipasti are served as starters before the pasta course. The title of this dish translates roughly as 'take your pick'.

Nutritional Information
Calories 378
Protein 43g
Carbohydrate 4g
Sugars 3g
Fat 22g
Saturates 6g

INGREDIENTS

200 g/7 oz canned tuna in oil, drained and
   flaked into chunks

115 g/4 oz canned sardines in oil, drained

100 g/3½ oz canned anchovy fillets in
   oil, drained

175 g/6 oz cooked peeled prawns, deveined

115 g/4 oz prosciutto, cut into strips

175 g/6 oz mozzarella cheese, sliced

390 g/13½ oz canned artichoke hearts,
   drained and halved lengthways

3 fresh figs, sliced

225 g/8 oz canned asparagus spears, drained

115 g/4 oz smoked salmon, thinly sliced

115 g/4 oz black olives

extra virgin olive oil, for drizzling

salt and pepper

lemon wedges, to garnish

1 Arrange the tuna, sardines, anchovies, prawns, prosciutto, mozzarella cheese, artichoke hearts and figs on a large serving platter.

2 Wrap 2–3 asparagus spears in each slice of smoked salmon and add to the platter. Season the antipasto to taste with salt and pepper.

3 Scatter the olives over the platter and drizzle with the olive oil. Garnish with lemon wedges, then serve immediately.

COOK'S TIP
Prosciutto is an Italian, salt-cured ham. The best-known variety is Parma ham from Parma, but other regions in Italy produce their own, such as San Daniele from Friuli.

10 mins

 10 mins

serves 6

20 MINUTES TO COOK

Bacon with Lamb's Lettuce

Lamb's lettuce, also known as corn salad and mâche, although it is neither true lettuce nor corn, has a sweet flavour that is perfectly complemented by crispy bacon and garlic croûtons.

Nutritional Information
Calories 270
Protein 8g
Carbohydrate 9g
Sugars 1g
Fat 23g
Saturates 5g

INGREDIENTS

6–8 tbsp sunflower oil

225 g/8 oz rindless streaky bacon, diced

2 garlic cloves, finely chopped

4 slices white bread, crusts removed,
    cut into 1-cm/½-inch cubes

5 tbsp red wine vinegar

1 tbsp balsamic vinegar

2 tsp wholegrain mustard

225 g/8 oz lamb's lettuce

salt and pepper

1 Heat 2 teaspoons of the sunflower oil in a large frying pan. Add the bacon and cook over a medium heat, stirring frequently, for 5 minutes, or until crisp. Remove from the frying pan with a slotted spoon and drain on kitchen paper. Add the garlic and diced bread to the frying pan and cook, stirring and tossing frequently, until crisp and golden brown on all sides. Remove from the frying pan with a slotted spoon and drain on kitchen paper.

2 Place the wine vinegar, balsamic vinegar, mustard and remaining sunflower oil in a screw-top jar and shake well to mix, then pour into a bowl. Alternatively, mix the vinegars and mustard together in a bowl and whisk in the sunflower oil until the dressing is creamy. Season to taste with salt and pepper.

3 Add the lamb's lettuce and bacon to the dressing and toss to coat. Divide the salad between serving plates, sprinkle with the croûtons and serve.

COOK'S TIP
Vinegars should be stored in a cool dark place because they lose most of their flavour if exposed to prolonged light and heat. They can be kept for at least six months.

5 mins

 15 mins

serves 4

20 MINUTES TO COOK

Spinach & Garlic Salad

This robust salad goes especially well with pasta dishes. Roasting the garlic gives it a deliciously sweet flavour. This dish is suitable for both vegetarians and vegans.

Nutritional Information
Calories 228
Protein 6g
Carbohydrate 3g
Sugars 2g
Fat 21g
Saturates 2g

INGREDIENTS

12 garlic cloves, unpeeled
4 tbsp olive oil
450 g/1 lb fresh baby spinach leaves
55 g/2 oz chopped walnuts or pine kernels
2 tbsp lemon juice
salt and pepper

1 Preheat the oven to 190°C/375°F/ Gas Mark 5. Place the garlic cloves in an ovenproof dish, add 2 tablespoons of the olive oil and toss to coat. Roast in the preheated oven for 15 minutes.

2 Transfer the garlic and olive oil to a large salad bowl. Add the spinach leaves, chopped walnuts, lemon juice and remaining olive oil. Toss well to coat and season to taste with salt and pepper.

3 Transfer the salad to individual dishes and serve immediately, while the garlic is still warm. Diners can squeeze the softened garlic out of the skins at the table.

VARIATION
Substitute young sorrel leaves for the baby spinach leaves to give this salad a delicious, lemony flavour.

Grapefruit & Cheese Salad

Fresh pink grapefruit segments, ripe avocados and sliced Italian dolcelatte cheese make a deliciously different salad combination.

Nutritional Information
Calories 390
Protein 13g
Carbohydrate 4g
Sugars 3g
Fat 36g
Saturates 13g

INGREDIENTS

½ cos lettuce

½ oakleaf lettuce

2 pink grapefruit

2 ripe avocados

175 g/6 oz dolcelatte cheese, thinly sliced

fresh basil sprigs, to garnish

DRESSING

4 tbsp olive oil

1 tbsp white wine vinegar

salt and pepper

1 Arrange the lettuce leaves on 4 serving plates or in a salad bowl.

2 Remove the peel and pith from the grapefruit with a sharp serrated knife, catching the grapefruit juice in a bowl.

3 Segment the grapefruit by cutting down each side of the membrane. Remove all the membrane. Arrange the segments on the serving plates.

4 Peel, stone and slice the avocados, dipping them in the grapefruit juice to prevent from going brown. Arrange the slices on the salad with the dolcelatte cheese.

5 To make the dressing, combine any remaining grapefruit juice with the olive oil and vinegar. Season to taste with salt and pepper, mixing thoroughly to combine.

6 Drizzle the dressing over the salads. Garnish with fresh basil sprigs and serve immediately.

COOK'S TIP
Pink grapefruit segments make a very attractive colour combination with the avocados, but ordinary grapefruit will work just as well. To help avocados to ripen, keep them at room temperature in a brown paper bag.

20 MINUTES TO COOK

Green Bean Salad with Feta

This fresh-tasting salad is flavoured with fresh coriander, a herb that resembles flat-leaf parsley in appearance, but tastes quite different.

Nutritional Information
Calories 275
Protein 6g
Carbohydrate 8g
Sugars 7g
Fat 25g
Saturates 6g

INGREDIENTS

350 g/12 oz green beans, trimmed

1 red onion, chopped

3–4 tbsp chopped fresh coriander

2 radishes, thinly sliced

75 g/2¾ oz feta cheese (drained weight), crumbled

1 tsp chopped fresh oregano or ½ tsp dried oregano, plus sprigs to garnish

2 tbsp red wine or fruit vinegar

5 tbsp extra virgin olive oil

3 ripe tomatoes, cut into wedges

pepper

1 Bring 5 cm/2 inches water to the boil in the base of a steamer or in a medium saucepan. Add the green beans to the top of the steamer or place them in a metal colander set over the saucepan of water. Cover and steam for 5 minutes until just tender.

2 Transfer the beans to a bowl and add the onion, coriander, radishes and feta.

3 Sprinkle the oregano over the salad, then grind pepper over to taste. Whisk the vinegar and olive oil together and then pour over the salad. Toss gently to mix well.

4 Transfer to a serving platter, surround with the tomato wedges, garnish with oregano sprigs and serve.

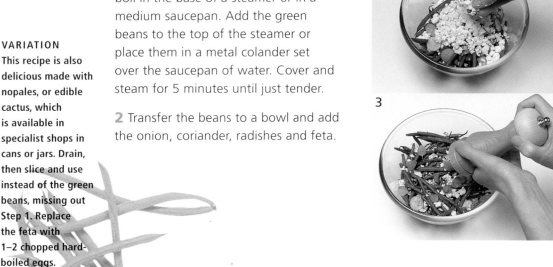

VARIATION
This recipe is also delicious made with nopales, or edible cactus, which is available in specialist shops in cans or jars. Drain, then slice and use instead of the green beans, missing out Step 1. Replace the feta with 1–2 chopped hard-boiled eggs.

74

20 MINUTES TO COOK Spinach Salad

Fresh baby spinach is tasty and light, and it makes an excellent and nutritious salad to go with the chicken and creamy dressing.

Nutritional Information

Calories 145

Protein 10g

Carbohydrate 4g

Sugars 3g

Fat 10g

Saturates 1g

INGREDIENTS

55 g/2 oz mushrooms

100 g/3½ oz baby spinach leaves, washed

85 g/3 oz radicchio leaves, shredded

100 g/3½ oz cooked skinless chicken breast fillet

55 g/2 oz Parma ham

2 tbsp olive oil

finely grated rind of ½ orange and juice of 1 orange

1 tbsp natural yogurt

salt and pepper

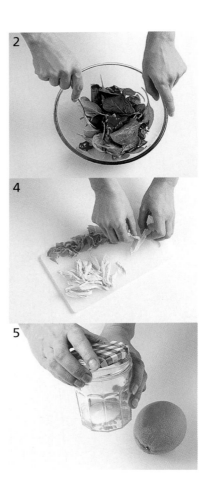

1 Wipe the mushrooms with a damp cloth or damp kitchen paper to remove any dirt.

2 Mix the spinach and radicchio together in a large salad bowl.

3 Using a sharp knife, thinly slice the mushrooms and add them to the salad bowl.

4 Shred the cooked chicken breast with your fingers and tear the Parma ham into strips. Mix them into the salad.

5 To make the dressing, place the olive oil, grated orange rind, orange juice and yogurt in a screw-top jar and shake to mix well. Season to taste with salt and pepper.

6 Drizzle the dressing over the spinach salad and toss until mixed. Serve.

VARIATION

Spinach is delicious when served raw. Try raw spinach in a salad garnished with bacon or garlicky croûtons. The young leaves have a wonderfully sharp flavour.

20 MINUTES TO COOK

Wild Mushroom Omelettes

Eggs are a great stand-by when time is short, but they don't have to be boring. An omelette with a creamy mushroom filling, perhaps served with a green salad, is a dish fit for a king.

Nutritional Information
Calories 457
Protein 21g
Carbohydrate 2g
Sugars 0g
Fat 41g
Saturates 21g

INGREDIENTS

25 g/1 oz butter
6 eggs, lightly beaten
salt and pepper
mixed salad, to serve
WILD MUSHROOM FILLING
25 g/1 oz butter
150 g/5½ oz wild mushrooms, sliced
2 tbsp crème fraîche

COOK'S TIP
Use whatever wild mushrooms are available, such as morels, chanterelles and flat or field mushrooms. To clean, rinse morels and chanterelles in cold water and shake dry. Wipe field mushrooms with a damp cloth.

1 To make the wild mushroom filling, heat the butter in a large, heavy-based frying pan. Add the mushrooms and cook over a low heat, stirring occasionally, for 5 minutes. Stir in the crème fraîche and season to taste with salt and pepper. Keep warm.

2 To make the omelettes, melt half the butter in an omelette pan or frying pan over a medium–high heat. Season the eggs to taste with salt and pepper, add half to the omelette pan and stir with a fork. As the egg sets, draw it towards the centre and tilt the pan so the uncooked egg runs underneath. Cook until the underside of the omelette is golden and set, but the top is moist.

3 Remove the omelette pan from the heat. Spoon half the mushroom mixture along a line just to one side of the centre of the omelette. Flip the other side over and slide the omelette onto a plate. Keep warm. Melt the remaining butter and cook a second omelette in the same way. Serve immediately with a mixed salad.

20 MINUTES TO COOK

Crab with Chinese Leaves

The delicate flavours of Chinese leaves and crabmeat are enhanced by the coconut milk in this recipe.

Nutritional Information
Calories 109
Protein 11g
Carbohydrate 2g
Sugars 1g
Fat 6g
Saturates 1g

INGREDIENTS

225 g/8 oz shiitake mushrooms
2 tbsp vegetable oil
2 garlic cloves, crushed
6 spring onions, sliced
1 head of Chinese leaves, shredded
1 tbsp mild curry paste
6 tbsp coconut milk
200 g/7 oz canned white crabmeat, drained
1 tsp red chilli flakes

1 Using a sharp knife, cut the mushrooms into slices.

2 Heat the vegetable oil in a large preheated wok or a frying pan with a heavy base.

3 Add the mushrooms and garlic to the wok or frying pan and stir-fry over a medium heat for 3 minutes, or until the mushrooms have softened.

4 Add the spring onions and shredded Chinese leaves to the wok and stir-fry for 10 minutes, or until the leaves have just wilted.

5 Mix the mild curry paste and coconut milk together in a small bowl.

6 Add the curry paste and coconut milk mixture to the wok, together with the crabmeat and chilli flakes. Mix together until thoroughly combined. Continue to heat the mixture in the wok until the juices begin to bubble.

7 Transfer the crab and vegetable stir-fry to warmed individual serving bowls and serve immediately.

COOK'S TIP
Shiitake mushrooms are now readily available in the fresh vegetable section of most large supermarkets.

Tabasco Steaks with Watercress Butter

20 MINUTES TO COOK

A variation on a classic theme, this simple, but rather extravagant dish would be ideal for a special occasion barbecue party.

Nutritional Information
Calories 462
Protein 53g
Carbohydrate 0g
Sugars 0g
Fat 28g
Saturates 16g

INGREDIENTS

1 bunch of watercress

85 g/3 oz unsalted butter, softened

4 sirloin steaks, about 225 g/8 oz each

4 tsp Tabasco sauce

salt and pepper

1 Preheat the barbecue. Using a sharp knife, finely chop enough watercress to fill 4 tablespoons. Reserve a few watercress leaves for the garnish. Place the butter in a small bowl and beat in the chopped watercress with a fork until fully incorporated. Cover with clingfilm and leave to chill in the refrigerator until required.

2 Sprinkle each steak with 1 teaspoon of the Tabasco sauce, rubbing it in well. Season to taste with salt and pepper.

3 Cook the steaks over hot coals for 2½ minutes each side for rare, 4 minutes each side for medium and 6 minutes each side for well done. Transfer to serving plates, garnish with the reserved watercress leaves and serve immediately, topped with the watercress butter.

VARIATION
If you like, substitute the same amount of fresh flat-leaf parsley for the watercress. Alternatively, serve the steaks with pesto.

82

20 MINUTES TO COOK

Spicy Tomato Chicken

These low-fat, spicy skewers are cooked in a matter of minutes – if you have time, assemble them in advance and leave to chill until needed.

Nutritional Information
Calories 195
Protein 28g
Carbohydrate 12g
Sugars 11g
Fat 4g
Saturates 1g

INGREDIENTS

500 g/1 lb 2 oz skinless, boneless chicken breasts
3 tbsp tomato purée
2 tbsp clear honey
2 tbsp Worcestershire sauce
1 tbsp chopped fresh rosemary
250 g/9 oz cherry tomatoes
fresh rosemary sprigs, to garnish
couscous, to serve

1 Preheat the grill to medium–high. Cut the chicken into 2.5-cm/1-inch chunks and place in a bowl.

2 Mix the tomato purée, honey, Worcestershire sauce and chopped rosemary together in a small bowl. Add to the chicken, stirring to coat evenly.

3 Alternating the chicken pieces and cherry tomatoes, thread them onto 8 metal or presoaked wooden skewers.

4 Spoon over any remaining glaze. Cook under the hot grill for 8–10 minutes, turning occasionally, until the chicken is thoroughly cooked.

5 Serve on a bed of couscous, garnished with rosemary sprigs.

1

2

3

COOK'S TIP
Couscous is made from semolina that has been formed into separate grains. It usually just needs moistening or steaming before serving.

20 MINUTES TO COOK

Blackened Chicken

Blackened dishes – seasoned and chargrilled – are synonymous with Cajun cooking, but are not traditional and were invented quite recently.

INGREDIENTS

4 skinless, boneless whole chicken breasts, about 175 g/6 oz each

2 tbsp natural yogurt

1 tbsp lemon juice

1 garlic clove, very finely chopped

1 tsp paprika

1 tsp ground cumin

1 tsp mustard powder

½ tsp dried thyme

½ tsp dried oregano

½ tsp cayenne pepper

sunflower oil, for brushing

TO GARNISH

thinly sliced onion rings

fresh flat-leaf parsley sprigs

VARIATION
If you like, substitute tuna steaks for the chicken, but don't cut them in half. Cook over medium hot coals for 4 minutes on each side, then serve immediately.

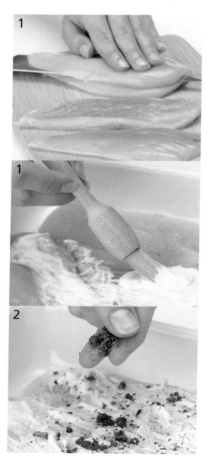

1 Preheat the barbecue. Slice the chicken breasts in half horizontally and flatten slightly with your hand. Place the chicken pieces in a large, shallow, non-metallic dish. Mix the yogurt and lemon juice together in a small bowl and brush the mixture over the chicken.

2 Mix the garlic, paprika, cumin, mustard powder, thyme, oregano and cayenne pepper together in a separate bowl and sprinkle the mixture evenly over the chicken.

3 Brush the chicken pieces with sunflower oil and cook over medium hot coals for 3 minutes on each side, or until beginning to blacken and the chicken is thoroughly cooked. Transfer to a serving plate and garnish with onion rings and parsley sprigs. Serve.

20 MINUTES TO COOK

Gammon in Madeira Sauce

This is an easy version of an old-fashioned recipe that involves rather more time and effort. It is just as delicious. Serve with freshly cooked vegetables for a tasty, nutritious supper.

3 Add the Madeira to the frying pan and bring to the boil, stirring and scraping up any sediment from the base of the frying pan. Stir in the mustard and cook for 2 minutes, or until the sauce is thickened and glossy.

4 Pour the Madeira sauce over the gammon, garnish with parsley sprigs and serve immediately.

Nutritional Information
Calories 493
Protein 67g
Carbohydrate 2g
Sugars 2g
Fat 18g
Saturates 8g

INGREDIENTS

4 gammon steaks, about 225 g/8 oz each

25 g/1 oz butter

2 cloves

1 mace blade

225 ml/8 fl oz Madeira

2 tsp Meaux mustard

fresh flat-leaf parsley sprigs, to garnish

1 Snip the edges of the gammon steaks with kitchen scissors to prevent them curling up as they cook.

2 Melt the butter in a large, heavy-based frying pan, then add the cloves and mace blade. Add the gammon, in batches if necessary, and cook for 3 minutes on each side. Transfer to a warmed dish, cover and keep warm.

COOK'S TIP
Mace is available in blades and ready ground. Try to buy blades because the ground powder deteriorates rapidly. Store mace blades in a cool place in an airtight container.

20 MINUTES TO COOK

Chicken & Mango Stir-fry

A colourful, exotic mix of flavours that works surprisingly well, this dish is easy and quick to cook – ideal for a midweek family meal.

Nutritional Information
Calories 200
Protein 23g
Carbohydrate 7g
Sugars 5g
Fat 6g
Saturates 1g

INGREDIENTS

6 skinless, boneless chicken thighs
2 tsp grated fresh root ginger
1 garlic clove, crushed
1 small fresh red chilli, deseeded and chopped
1 large red pepper, deseeded
4 spring onions
200 g/7 oz mangetout
100 g/3½ oz baby corn cobs
1 large ripe mango
2 tbsp sunflower oil
1 tbsp light soy sauce
3 tbsp rice wine or sherry
1 tsp sesame oil
salt and pepper
snipped fresh chives, to garnish

1 Cut the chicken into long, thin strips and place in a bowl. Combine the ginger, garlic and chilli, then stir the mixture into the chicken strips to coat them evenly.

2 Slice the pepper thinly, cutting diagonally. Trim and diagonally slice the spring onions. Cut the mangetout and corn cobs in half diagonally. Peel the mango, remove the stone and slice thinly.

3 Heat the sunflower oil in a large, heavy-based frying pan or preheated wok over a high heat. Add the chicken and stir-fry for 4–5 minutes, or until just turning golden brown. Add the pepper slices and stir-fry over a medium heat for 4–5 minutes, or until softened.

4 Add the spring onions, mangetout and corn cobs and stir-fry for a further 1 minute.

5 Mix the soy sauce, rice wine and sesame oil together, then stir the mixture into the wok. Add the mango slices and stir gently for 1 minute, or until heated through.

6 Season to taste with salt and pepper, garnish with snipped fresh chives and serve immediately.

20 MINUTES TO COOK   Tarragon Turkey

This economical dish is quick and simple to prepare, and yet it tastes absolutely wonderful, not least because poultry and tarragon have a natural affinity.

Nutritional Information
Calories 296
Protein 48g
Carbohydrate 0g
Sugars 1g
Fat 11g
Saturates 4g

INGREDIENTS

4 turkey breasts, about 175 g/6 oz each

4 tsp wholegrain mustard

8 fresh tarragon sprigs, plus extra to garnish

4 smoked back bacon rashers

salt and pepper

salad leaves, to serve

1 Preheat the barbecue. Season the turkey breasts to taste with salt and pepper, and, using a round-bladed knife, spread the mustard evenly over the turkey.

2 Place 2 tarragon sprigs on top of each turkey breast and wrap a bacon rasher around it to hold the herbs in place. Secure with a cocktail stick.

3 Cook the turkey over medium hot coals for 5–8 minutes on each side, or until thoroughly cooked. Transfer to serving plates and garnish with tarragon sprigs. Serve with salad leaves.

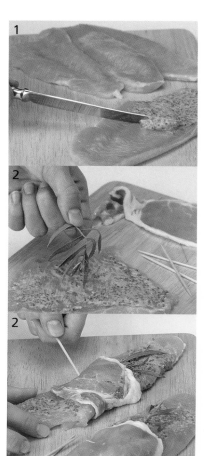

COOK'S TIP
Make sure you buy genuine French tarragon, as Russian tarragon is coarse and can taste unpleasant. It is not worth using dried tarragon, which has an insipid flavour.

20 MINUTES TO COOK

Oyster Sauce Lamb

This really is a speedy dish, lamb leg steaks being perfect for the short cooking time.

Nutritional Information
Calories 243
Protein 26g
Carbohydrate 3g
Sugars 0.4g
Fat 14g
Saturates 5g

INGREDIENTS

450 g/1 lb lamb leg steaks
1 tsp ground Szechuan peppercorns
1 tbsp groundnut oil
2 garlic cloves
8 spring onions
2 tbsp dark soy sauce
6 tbsp oyster sauce
175 g/6 oz Chinese leaves

1 Using a sharp knife, remove any excess fat from the lamb. Slice the lamb into thin strips and place in a bowl.

2 Sprinkle the ground Szechuan peppercorns over the meat and toss together until well combined.

3 Heat the groundnut oil in a preheated wok or large, heavy-based frying pan.

4 Add the lamb to the wok and stir-fry for 5 minutes.

5 Meanwhile, crush the garlic cloves in a mortar with a pestle or with a garlic crusher and slice the spring onions. Add the garlic and spring onions to the wok together with the soy sauce and stir-fry for 2 minutes.

COOK'S TIP
Oyster sauce is made from oysters, which are cooked in brine and soy sauce. Sold in bottles, it will keep in the refrigerator for months.

2

4

5

6 Add the oyster sauce and Chinese leaves and stir-fry for a further 2 minutes, or until the leaves have wilted and the juices are bubbling.

7 Transfer the stir-fry to warmed serving bowls and serve hot.

20 MINUTES TO COOK Cod & Tomato Parcels

Cooking cod steaks in this way keeps the flesh deliciously moist and succulent and seals in the flavour of the herbed tomatoes. White wine gives the parcels an added richness.

Nutritional Information
Calories 173
Protein 31g
Carbohydrate 3g
Sugars 3g
Fat 3g
Saturates 1g

INGREDIENTS

4 cod steaks, about 175 g/6 oz each

2 tsp extra virgin olive oil

4 tomatoes, peeled and chopped

25 g/1 oz fresh basil leaves, torn into small pieces

4 tbsp white wine

salt and pepper

1 Preheat the barbecue. Rinse the cod steaks under cold running water and pat dry with kitchen paper. Using a sharp knife, cut out and discard the central bones. Cut out 4 rectangles, 33 x 20 cm/13 x 8 inches, from double-thickness foil and brush with the olive oil. Place a cod steak in the centre of each piece of foil.

2 Mix the tomatoes, basil and white wine together in a bowl and season to taste with salt and pepper. Spoon the tomato mixture equally on top of the fish. Bring up the sides of the foil and fold over securely.

3 Cook the cod parcels over hot coals for 3–5 minutes on each side, or until cooked. Transfer to 4 large serving plates and serve in the parcels.

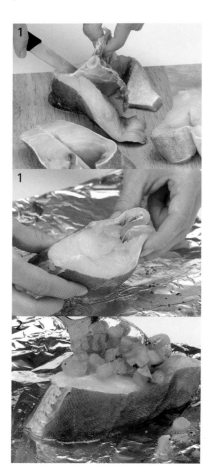

COOK'S TIP

For an attractive presentation, unwrap the parcels and slide the contents, tomato-side upwards, onto warmed serving plates. Remove and discard the skin from the outside of the cod steaks before serving.

Grilled Scallops & Prawns with Citrus Butter

20 MINUTES TO COOK

Seafood and citrus fruit have a natural affinity with each other and this dish will taste equally delicious whether you use limes or lemons to flavour the butter. Unpeeled prawns look attractive, but you can peel them, if you like.

Nutritional Information

Calories 337
Protein 25g
Carbohydrate 9g
Sugars 4g
Fat 23g
Saturates 13g

INGREDIENTS

12 thawed prepared scallops

12 raw tiger prawns

finely grated rind and juice of 1 lime or lemon

1 egg yolk

6 tbsp melted butter

1 tbsp snipped fresh dill or chopped fresh chervil

2 red onions, cut into wedges

olive oil, for brushing

salt and pepper

1 Preheat the grill to medium. Place the scallops and prawns in a large, shallow, non-metallic dish, add half the lime rind and half the juice and toss well.

2 Beat the egg yolk with the remaining lime rind and juice in a small bowl. Gradually whisk in the melted butter, 1 tablespoon at a time. Continue to whisk until the mixture is thick and smooth. Stir in the dill and season to taste with salt and pepper.

3 Brush the onion wedges with olive oil and cook under the hot grill for 5 minutes, turning them once. Meanwhile, thread the scallops and prawns onto several metal or presoaked wooden skewers, place them under the grill and cook for 1½–2 minutes on each side, or until the scallops become opaque and the prawns have changed colour.

4 Remove the seafood from the skewers and place on a warmed serving plate. Surround them with the onion wedges, pour the citrus butter over them and serve.

COOK'S TIP
If using wooden skewers, soak them in warm water for 30 minutes, drain, pat dry, then thread the food onto them. Soaking prevents the skewers burning under the grill.

8 mins

serves 4

20 MINUTES TO COOK Thai Fragrant Mussels

Lemon grass, galangal and lime leaves delicately flavour and perfume this simple and elegant dish. Serve with a chilli sauce for dipping, if you like.

Nutritional Information
Calories 133
Protein 26g
Carbohydrate 1g
Sugars 0g.
Fat 3g
Saturates 1g

INGREDIENTS

2 kg/4 lb 8 oz live mussels, scrubbed and debearded

2 lemon grass stalks, lightly crushed

5-cm/2-inch piece galangal or fresh root ginger, bruised

5 kaffir lime leaves, shredded

3 garlic cloves

300 ml/10 fl oz water

salt

1 Discard any mussels with broken or damaged shells and any that refuse to close immediately when sharply tapped with the back of a knife. Rinse under cold running water.

2 Place the mussels, lemon grass, galangal, lime leaves, garlic and water in a flameproof casserole or large saucepan and season to taste with salt. Bring to the boil, then cover and cook over a high heat, shaking the saucepan occasionally, for 5 minutes, or until the shells have opened.

3 Remove and discard the flavourings and any mussels that remain closed. Divide the mussels between 4 soup bowls with a slotted spoon. Tilt the casserole to let any sand settle, then spoon the cooking liquid over the mussels and serve immediately.

COOK'S TIP
Galangal is used extensively in South-east Asia. It is a member of the ginger family, but is spicier than fresh root ginger. It can be found in Asian food shops. If it is unavailable, then use fresh root ginger instead.

Moules Marinières

This classic recipe is a shellfish-lover's feast. To make it into a perfect meal, the only extra treat you need is a glass of white wine.

Nutritional Information

Calories 185
Protein 26g
Carbohydrate 2g
Sugars 1g
Fat 3g
Saturates 1g

INGREDIENTS

2 kg/4 lb 8 oz live mussels

300 ml/10 fl oz dry white wine

6 shallots, finely chopped

1 bouquet garni

pepper

bay leaves, to garnish

1 Clean the mussels by scrubbing or scraping the shells and pulling off any beards. Discard any with broken or damaged shells or any that refuse to close when tapped with a knife. Rinse the mussels under cold running water.

2 Meanwhile, pour the wine into a large, heavy-based saucepan, add the shallots and bouquet garni and season to taste with pepper. Bring to the boil over a medium heat. Add the mussels, cover tightly and cook, shaking the saucepan occasionally, for 5 minutes. Remove and discard the bouquet garni and any mussels that remain closed.

3 Divide the mussels between 4 soup bowls with a slotted spoon. Tilt the saucepan to let any sand settle, then spoon the cooking liquid over the mussels, garnish with bay leaves and serve immediately.

COOK'S TIP
Never eat mussels that you have collected from the beach yourself, as they may have been polluted and could cause serious illness.

10 mins

10 mins

serves 4

20 MINUTES TO COOK

Herrings with Hot Pesto

Oily fish, such as herrings and mackerel, form a vital part of the healthy diet, because they are rich in essential omega-3 fatty acids.

Nutritional Information
Calories 382
Protein 28g
Carbohydrate 3g
Sugars 2g
Fat 29g
Saturates 5g

INGREDIENTS

4 herrings or small mackerel, cleaned and gutted

2 tbsp olive oil

225 g/8 oz tomatoes, peeled, deseeded and chopped

8 canned anchovy fillets in oil, drained and chopped

about 30 fresh basil leaves

55 g/2 oz pine kernels

2 garlic cloves, crushed

1 Preheat the grill. Cook the herrings or mackerel under the hot grill for 8–10 minutes on each side, or until the skin is slightly charred on both sides.

2 Meanwhile, heat 1 tablespoon of the olive oil in a large saucepan. Add the tomatoes and anchovies and cook over a medium heat for 5 minutes.

3 To make the pesto sauce, place the basil, pine kernels, garlic and remaining olive oil in a food processor and process to form a smooth paste. Alternatively, pound the ingredients by hand in a mortar with a pestle.

4 Add the pesto mixture to the saucepan of tomato and anchovy and stir to heat through.

5 Spoon some of the pesto sauce onto 4 warmed individual serving plates. Place the fish on top and pour the rest of the pesto sauce over the fish. Serve immediately.

20 MINUTES TO COOK Cajun-spiced Fish

Descended from immigrant French cuisine, Cajun cooking is marked with a practical approach that makes the most of the locally available ingredients in the countryside around New Orleans.

Nutritional Information
Calories 215
Protein 33g
Carbohydrate 2g
Sugars 2g
Fat 8g
Saturates 2g

INGREDIENTS

1 tbsp lime juice

2 tbsp low-fat natural yogurt

4 swordfish steaks, about 175 g/6 oz each

sunflower or corn oil, for brushing

lemon wedges, to garnish

SPICE MIX

1 tsp paprika

1 tsp cayenne pepper

1 tsp ground cumin

1 tsp mustard powder

1 tsp dried oregano

1 First make the spice mix by blending all the ingredients together in a bowl. Mix the lime juice and yogurt together in a separate bowl.

2 Pat the fish steaks dry with kitchen paper, then brush both sides with the yogurt mixture. Use your hands to coat both sides of the fish with the spice mix, rubbing it well into the flesh.

3 Brush a griddle pan with a little sunflower oil and heat over a medium heat. Add the fish steaks and cook for 5 minutes, then turn over and cook for a further 4 minutes, or until the flesh flakes easily when tested with a fork. Serve straight from the griddle pan garnished with lemon wedges.

COOK'S TIP
Brush the fish steaks lightly with oil and cook under a preheated hot grill or on a barbecue instead. Brush again with oil when you turn them.

106

Griddled Squid

20 MINUTES TO COOK

This recipe works best with delicate baby squid, but if you can obtain only larger squid, slice the bodies into thick rings and cut the tentacles in half before you begin cooking.

Nutritional Information
Calories 137
Protein 18g
Carbohydrate 1g
Sugars 0g
Fat 7g
Saturates 1g

INGREDIENTS

450 g/1 lb baby squid
2 tbsp olive oil
1 bunch of fresh parsley, finely chopped
4 garlic cloves, crushed
1 tbsp grated lemon rind
1 tbsp lemon juice
salt and pepper
fresh flat-leaf parsley sprigs, to garnish

1 To prepare each squid, pull the pouch and tentacles apart, then remove the remaining innards from the pouch. Slice the tentacles away from the head and discard the head. Rinse the pouch and tentacles under cold running water.

2 Heat a griddle pan and brush with olive oil. Add the squid pouches and tentacles and cook over a medium heat, turning and brushing with more oil occasionally, for 5–10 minutes, or until golden brown. Divide between 4 serving plates.

3 Place the parsley, garlic and lemon rind in a small bowl and stir to mix. Sprinkle the lemon juice over the squid and season to taste with salt and pepper. Sprinkle the parsley mixture over the squid, garnish with parsley sprigs and serve warm.

COOK'S TIP
If you don't want to use a griddle pan for this dish, you can also cook the squid under a preheated hot grill, turning frequently and brushing with olive oil.

108

20 MINUTES TO COOK Sweet & Sour Tofu

Sweet-and-sour sauce was one of the first Chinese sauces introduced to Western diets and remains one of the most popular.

Nutritional Information
Calories 205
Protein 11g
Carbohydrate 17g
Sugars 12g
Fat 11g
Saturates 1g

INGREDIENTS

2 celery sticks

1 carrot

1 green pepper, deseeded

85 g/3 oz mangetout

2 tbsp vegetable oil

2 garlic cloves, crushed

8 baby corn cobs

115 g/4 oz beansprouts

450 g/1 lb firm tofu (drained weight), cubed

SAUCE

2 tbsp light brown sugar

2 tbsp wine vinegar

225 ml/8 fl oz vegetable stock

1 tsp tomato purée

1 tbsp cornflour

1 Using a sharp knife, thinly slice the celery, cut the carrot into thin strips, dice the pepper and cut the mangetout in half diagonally.

2 Heat the vegetable oil in a preheated wok until it is almost smoking. Reduce the heat slightly, add the crushed garlic, celery, carrot, pepper, mangetout and baby corn cobs and stir-fry for 3–4 minutes.

3 Add the beansprouts and tofu to the wok and cook for 2 minutes, stirring frequently.

4 To make the sauce, combine the sugar, vinegar, vegetable stock, tomato purée and cornflour, stirring well to mix. Stir into the wok, bring to the boil and cook, stirring constantly, until the sauce thickens and clears. Continue to cook for 1 minute. Transfer to a warmed serving dish or bowl and serve immediately.

COOK'S TIP
Be careful not to break up the tofu cubes when stirring.

20 MINUTES TO COOK   # Thai-spiced Mushrooms

An unusual dish that makes a good vegetarian main course. Serve the mushrooms with a colourful fresh salad, if you like.

Nutritional Information
Calories 147
Protein 6g
Carbohydrate 4g
Sugars 2g
Fat 12g
Saturates 1g

INGREDIENTS

8 large, flat mushrooms

3 tbsp sunflower oil

2 tbsp light soy sauce

1 garlic clove, crushed

2-cm/³/₄-inch piece fresh galangal or root ginger, grated

1 tbsp Thai green curry paste

8 baby corn cobs, sliced

3 spring onions, chopped

115 g/4 oz beansprouts

100 g/3½ oz firm tofu (drained weight), diced

2 tsp sesame seeds, toasted

TO SERVE

chopped cucumber

sliced red pepper

1 Preheat the grill. Remove the stalks from the mushrooms and reserve. Place the caps on a baking sheet. Mix 2 tablespoons of the sunflower oil with 1 tablespoon of the soy sauce and brush all over the mushroom caps.

2 Cook the mushroom caps under the hot grill until golden and tender, turning them over once.

3 Meanwhile, chop the mushroom stalks finely. Heat the remaining oil in a heavy-based frying pan or preheated wok and stir-fry the stalks with the garlic and galangal for 1 minute.

4 Stir in the curry paste, baby corn cobs and spring onions and stir-fry for 1 minute. Add the beansprouts and stir-fry for a further 1 minute.

5 Add the tofu and remaining soy sauce, then toss lightly to heat through. Carefully spoon the mixture into the mushroom caps.

6 Sprinkle with the sesame seeds. Serve immediately with chopped cucumber and sliced red pepper.

COOK'S TIP
Galangal and root ginger can be frozen for several weeks, either peeled and finely chopped ready to add to dishes, or in whole pieces. Thaw the piece or grate finely from frozen.

20 MINUTES TO COOK

Hot & Crispy Noodles

These crispy noodles will add a delicious crunch to your Chinese meal. They can be served as a side dish or as an appetizer for people to share.

Nutritional Information

Calories 104
Protein 2g
Carbohydrate 11g
Sugars 0.3g
Fat 6g
Saturates 1g

INGREDIENTS

250 g/9 oz rice noodles

vegetable oil, for deep-frying

2 garlic cloves, finely chopped

8 spring onions, finely chopped

1 small fresh red or green chilli, deseeded and finely chopped

2 tbsp Thai fish sauce

2 tbsp light soy sauce

2 tbsp lime or lemon juice

2 tbsp molasses sugar

TO GARNISH

spring onions, shredded

cucumber, thinly sliced

fresh chillies

1 Break the noodles into smaller pieces with your hands. Heat the vegetable oil for deep-frying in a wok or large frying pan and deep-fry small batches of the noodles until pale golden brown and puffed up. Lift the noodles out with a slotted spoon and leave to drain on kitchen paper.

2 When all of the noodles are cooked, pour off the oil, leaving 3 tablespoons in the wok. Add the garlic, spring onions and chopped chilli, and stir-fry for 2 minutes.

3 Mix the fish sauce, soy sauce, lime juice and sugar together. Add to the wok and cook for 2 minutes, or until the sugar has dissolved. Tip all the noodles back into the wok and toss lightly to coat with the sauce mixture.

4 Serve the noodles garnished with shredded spring onions, thinly sliced cucumber and chillies.

VARIATION

Stir-fry some uncooked peeled prawns or chopped raw chicken with the spring onions and garlic in Step 2. Cook for an extra 3–4 minutes to make sure they are thoroughly cooked.

12 mins

 8 mins

serves 4

20 MINUTES TO COOK

Seasonal Stir-fry

When selecting different fresh vegetables for this dish, bear in mind that there should always be a contrast in colour as well as texture.

Nutritional Information
Calories 108
Protein 3g
Carbohydrate 4g
Sugars 3g
Fat 9g
Saturates 1g

INGREDIENTS

1 red pepper, deseeded

115 g/4 oz courgettes

115 g/4 oz cauliflower

115 g/4 oz French beans

3 tbsp vegetable oil

few small slices of fresh root ginger

½ tsp salt

½ tsp sugar

1–2 tbsp vegetable stock or water (optional)

1 tbsp light soy sauce

few drops of sesame oil (optional)

1 Using a sharp knife or Chinese cleaver, cut the red pepper into small squares. Thinly slice the courgettes. Trim the cauliflower and divide into small florets, discarding any thick stems. Make sure all the vegetables are cut into roughly similar shapes and sizes to ensure that they cook evenly. Trim the French beans, then cut them in half.

2 Heat the vegetable oil in a preheated wok or large, heavy-based frying pan. Add the prepared vegetables with the ginger and stir-fry for 2 minutes.

3 Add the salt and sugar to the wok and continue to stir-fry for 1–2 minutes, adding a little vegetable stock if the mixture appears to be too dry. Do not add any liquid unless necessary.

4 Add the soy sauce and sesame oil, if using, and stir well to coat the vegetables lightly.

5 Transfer the stir-fried vegetables to a warmed serving dish or bowl and serve immediately.

VARIATION
Almost any vegetables could be used in this dish, but make sure there is a good variety of colour, and always include several crisp vegetables, such as carrots or mangetout.

1

2

20 MINUTES TO COOK

Summer Fruit Salad

A mixture of soft summer fruits in an orange-flavoured syrup with a dash of port. Serve with low-fat fromage frais.

Nutritional Information
Calories 110
Protein 1g
Carbohydrate 26g
Sugars 26g
Fat 0.1g
Saturates 0g

INGREDIENTS

85 g/3 oz caster sugar

5 tbsp water

grated rind and juice of 1 small orange

250 g/9 oz redcurrants, stripped from their stalks

2 tsp arrowroot

2 tbsp port

115 g/4 oz blackberries

115 g/4 oz blueberries

115 g/4 oz strawberries

225 g/8 oz raspberries

fresh mint sprigs, to decorate (optional)

low-fat fromage frais, to serve

1 Place the sugar, water and grated orange rind in a heavy-based saucepan and heat gently, stirring until the sugar has dissolved.

2 Add the redcurrants and orange juice, bring to the boil and simmer gently for 2–3 minutes.

3 Sieve the fruit through a non-metallic sieve, reserving the syrup, and place in a bowl.

4 Blend the arrowroot with a little water. Return the syrup to the saucepan, add the arrowroot and bring to the boil, stirring until thickened.

5 Add the port and mix together well. Then pour the syrup over the redcurrants in the bowl.

6 Add the blackberries, blueberries, strawberries and raspberries. Mix the fruit together and leave to cool until required. Transfer to individual glass dishes, decorate with mint sprigs, if using, and serve with a spoonful of low-fat fromage frais.

COOK'S TIP
Although this salad is really best made with fresh fruits in season, you can achieve an acceptable result with frozen equivalents, with perhaps the exception of strawberries. You can buy frozen fruits of the forest, which would be ideal, in most supermarkets.

Peaches & Mascarpone

If you have time and prepare these in advance, all you have to do is pop the peaches on the barbecue when you are ready to serve them.

Nutritional Information
Calories 301
Protein 6g
Carbohydrate 24g
Sugars 24g
Fat 20g
Saturates 9g

INGREDIENTS

4 peaches

175 g/6 oz mascarpone cheese

40 g/1½ oz pecan nuts or walnuts, chopped

1 tsp sunflower oil

4 tbsp maple syrup

1 Preheat the barbecue. Cut the peaches in half and remove the stones.

2 Mix the mascarpone and nuts together in a small bowl until well combined. Cover and leave to chill in the refrigerator until required.

3 Brush the peaches with a little sunflower oil and place on a rack set over medium hot coals. Barbecue for 5–10 minutes, turning once, until hot.

4 Transfer the peaches to a serving dish and top with the mascarpone mixture. Drizzle the maple syrup over the top and serve immediately.

1

2

3

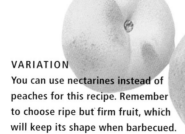

VARIATION
You can use nectarines instead of peaches for this recipe. Remember to choose ripe but firm fruit, which will keep its shape when barbecued.

20 MINUTES TO COOK

Poached Allspice Pears

These pears are moist and delicious after poaching in a sugar and allspice mixture. They are wonderful served hot or cold.

Nutritional Information
Calories 157
Protein 5g
Carbohydrate 17g
Sugars 17g
Fat 19g
Saturates 12g

INGREDIENTS

4 large, ripe pears
300 ml/10 fl oz orange juice
2 tsp ground allspice
55 g/2 oz raisins
2 tbsp light brown sugar
finely pared orange zest, to decorate

1 Using an apple corer, core the pears, then using a sharp knife, peel the pears and cut them in half.

2 Place the pear halves in a large saucepan.

3 Add the orange juice, allspice, raisins and sugar to the saucepan and heat gently, stirring, until the sugar has dissolved. Bring the mixture to the boil for 1 minute.

4 Reduce the heat to low and leave to simmer for 10 minutes, or until the pears are cooked, but still fairly firm.

5 Remove the pears from the saucepan with a slotted spoon and transfer to serving plates. Decorate with orange zest and serve hot with the syrup.

COOK'S TIP
Do not use over-ripe pears for this dessert because they will become mushy and fall apart when cooked. The best way to test if the pears are cooked, but still fairly firm, is to insert the point of a sharp knife into the flesh of the pears.

30 minutes to cook

If you are looking for a delicious, low-carbohydrate meal that can be prepared, cooked and served in just 30 minutes, then a recipe from this section is perfect. Beef Kebabs, Thai Prawn Curry and Totally Tropical Pineapple are just a few of the tasty dishes.

30 MINUTES TO COOK   Chinese Vegetable Soup

This deliciously fresh vegetable broth would make an unusual first course for a dinner party or a tasty light lunch. Its Oriental ingredients lend an Eastern flavour to the marinated tofu. The soup is suitable for both vegetarians and vegans.

Nutritional Information
Calories 117
Protein 6g
Carbohydrate 5g
Sugars 3g
Fat 8g
Saturates 1g

INGREDIENTS

115 g/4 oz Chinese leaves

2 tbsp groundnut oil

225 g/8 oz marinated tofu (drained weight), cut into 1-cm/1/2-inch cubes

2 garlic cloves, thinly sliced

4 spring onions, diagonally thinly sliced

1 carrot, thinly sliced

1 litre/13/4 pints vegetable stock

1 tbsp Chinese rice wine

2 tbsp light soy sauce

1 tsp sugar

salt and pepper

1 Shred the Chinese leaves and reserve. Heat the groundnut oil in a large preheated wok or frying pan. Add the tofu cubes and stir-fry for 4–5 minutes, or until browned, then remove from the wok with a slotted spoon and drain on kitchen paper.

2 Add the garlic, spring onions and carrot to the wok and stir-fry for 2 minutes. Pour in the vegetable stock, rice wine and soy sauce, then add the sugar and shredded Chinese leaves. Cook over a medium heat for 1–2 minutes, or until heated through.

3 Season to taste with salt and pepper and add the tofu. Ladle the soup into warmed bowls and serve.

COOK'S TIP
Always use a very sharp knife when cutting tofu because it is soft and easily squashed. A blunt knife will produce unevenly shaped cubes.

30 MINUTES TO COOK Aubergines with Tsatziki

This makes a delicious starter for a summer barbecue lunch or can be served as part of a vegetarian barbecue meze with other crudités, dips and salads of your choice.

Nutritional Information
Calories 137
Protein 5g
Carbohydrate 5g
Sugars 5g
Fat 11g
Saturates 4g

INGREDIENTS

2 tbsp olive oil

2 aubergines, thinly sliced

TSATZIKI

½ cucumber

200 ml/7 fl oz natural Greek yogurt

4 spring onions, finely chopped

1 garlic clove, finely chopped

3 tbsp chopped fresh mint

salt and pepper

1 fresh mint sprig, to garnish

1 Preheat the barbecue. To make the tsatziki, finely chop the cucumber. Place the yogurt in a bowl and beat well until smooth. Stir in the cucumber, spring onions, garlic and mint. Season to taste with salt and pepper. Transfer to a small serving bowl, cover with clingfilm and leave to chill in the refrigerator until required.

2 Season the olive oil with salt and pepper, then brush the aubergine slices with the oil.

3 Cook the aubergines over hot coals for 5 minutes on each side, brushing with more olive oil, if necessary. Transfer to a large serving plate and serve immediately with the tsatziki, garnished with a mint sprig.

COOK'S TIP

An alternative dip to serve with the aubergines can be made by blending 300 ml/10 fl oz soured cream with 2 crushed garlic cloves. Season with salt and pepper and chill before serving.

30 MINUTES TO COOK

Laksa

Ginger gives this dish its curative properties and also improves digestion and circulation. It is anti-inflammatory and can help to alleviate many common ailments.

Nutritional Information

Calories 157
Protein 20g
Carbohydrate 8.1g
Sugars 2.1g
Fat 5.2g
Saturates 0.8g

INGREDIENTS

1 tbsp sunflower oil

2–3 garlic cloves, cut into thin slivers

1–2 fresh red bird's eye chillies, deseeded and sliced

2 lemon grass stalks, outer leaves removed, chopped

2.5-cm/1-inch piece fresh root ginger, grated

1.2 litres/2 pints fish or vegetable stock

350 g/12 oz large raw prawns, peeled and deveined

115 g/4 oz shiitake mushrooms, sliced

1 large carrot, grated

55 g/2 oz dried egg noodles (optional)

1–2 tsp Thai fish sauce

1 tbsp chopped fresh coriander

1 Heat the sunflower oil in a saucepan over a medium heat, add the garlic, chillies, lemon grass and ginger and cook for 5 minutes. Add the fish stock and bring to the boil, then reduce the heat and simmer for 5 minutes.

2 Stir in the prawns, mushrooms and carrot. If using the egg noodles, break into small lengths, add to the saucepan and simmer for 5 minutes, or until the prawns have turned pink and the noodles are tender.

3 Stir in the fish sauce and chopped coriander and heat through for a further 1 minute before serving in large soup bowls.

30 MINUTES TO COOK   Warm Tuna Salad

This colourful, refreshing first course is perfect for a special occasion. The dressing can be made in advance and spooned over just before serving.

Nutritional Information
Calories 127
Protein 13g
Carbohydrate 6g
Sugars 4g
Fat 5g
Saturates 1g

COOK'S TIP
You can make a quick version of this dish using canned tuna. Just drain and flake the tuna, omit Steps 2 and 3 and continue as in the recipe.

INGREDIENTS

55 g/2 oz Chinese leaves, shredded

3 tbsp Chinese rice wine

2 tbsp Thai fish sauce

1 tbsp finely shredded fresh root ginger

1 garlic clove, finely chopped

½ small fresh red bird's eye chilli, finely chopped

2 tsp soft light brown sugar

2 tbsp lime juice

400 g/14 oz fresh tuna steak

sunflower oil, for brushing

125 g/4½ oz cherry tomatoes

TO GARNISH

chopped fresh mint leaves

fresh mint sprigs

1 Place a small pile of shredded Chinese leaves on a serving plate. Place the rice wine, fish sauce, ginger, garlic, chilli, brown sugar and 1 tablespoon of the lime juice in a screw-top jar and shake well to mix.

2 Cut the tuna into strips of an even thickness. Sprinkle with the remaining lime juice.

3 Brush a ridged griddle pan or wide frying pan with the sunflower oil and heat until very hot. Arrange the tuna strips in the pan and cook until just firm and light golden, turning them over once. Remove and reserve.

4 Add the tomatoes to the griddle pan and cook over a high heat until lightly browned. Spoon the tuna and tomatoes over the Chinese leaves and spoon over the dressing. Garnish with chopped fresh mint and mint sprigs and serve warm.

30 MINUTES TO COOK

Lobster & Avocado Salad

This isn't really a main course dish but would serve very well as a light lunch with some or as part of a buffet party.

Nutritional Information

Calories 313
Protein 19g
Carbohydrate 4g
Sugars 3g
Fat 25g
Saturates 4g

INGREDIENTS

2 x 400 g/14 oz cooked lobsters
1 large avocado
1 tbsp lemon juice
225 g/8 oz green beans
4 spring onions, thinly sliced
2 tbsp chopped fresh chervil
1 tbsp snipped fresh chives

DRESSING

1 garlic clove, crushed
1 tsp Dijon mustard
pinch of sugar
1 tbsp balsamic vinegar
5 tbsp olive oil
salt and pepper

1 To prepare the lobsters, cut them in half lengthways. Remove the intestinal vein, which runs down the tail, the stomach sac and any grey beards from the body cavity at the head end of the lobster. Crack the claws and remove the meat – in 1 piece if possible. Remove the meat from the tail of the lobster. Roughly chop all the meat and reserve until required.

2 Split the avocado lengthways and remove the stone. Cut each half in half again and peel away the skin. Cut the avocado flesh into chunks and toss with the lemon juice to prevent it discolouring. Add to the lobster meat.

3 Bring a large saucepan of lightly salted water to the boil and add the green beans. Cook for 3 minutes, then drain and immediately refresh under cold running water. Drain again and leave to cool completely. Cut the beans in half, then add them to the avocado and lobster.

4 Meanwhile, make the dressing by whisking the garlic, mustard, sugar, vinegar and salt and pepper to taste together in a bowl. Gradually add the olive oil, whisking, until thickened.

5 Add the spring onions, chervil and chives to the lobster and avocado mixture and toss gently together. Drizzle over the dressing and serve the salad immediately.

30 MINUTES TO COOK

Stuffed Tomatoes

Tomatoes and anchovies taste wonderful together and make a delicious, light meal. Serve hot or warm in the Mediterranean style.

Nutritional Information
Calories 100
Protein 5g
Carbohydrate 8g
Sugars 5g
Fat 6g
Saturates 1g

INGREDIENTS

4 large tomatoes

8 canned anchovy fillets, drained and finely chopped

25 g/1 oz fresh white breadcrumbs

1 garlic clove, finely chopped

1 tbsp olive oil

1 egg, lightly beaten

salt and pepper

crisp green salad, to serve

1 Preheat the oven to 190°C/375°F/ Gas Mark 5. Using a sharp knife, slice the tops from the tomatoes and reserve. Scoop out the flesh with a teaspoon and reserve. Stand the tomato shells upside down on kitchen paper to drain.

2 Mix the anchovies, breadcrumbs, garlic, olive oil and enough of the egg to bind the mixture together in a small bowl. Season to taste with salt and pepper.

3 Spoon the filling into the tomato shells and replace the tops. Arrange the tomatoes in a large ovenproof dish and bake in the preheated oven for 20 minutes. Transfer to a large serving plate and serve hot or warm with a crisp green salad.

COOK'S TIP

Beef tomatoes are ideal for filling, as they are large and have a wonderful flavour. They should be ripe but firm, to ensure that they hold their shape when stuffed and baked.

30 MINUTES TO COOK   Broccoli & Sesame Frittata

Sesame seeds are one of the richest sources of phytosterols, plant chemicals that can be absorbed into the bloodstream and remove the cholesterol that has built up there.

Nutritional Information
Calories 415
Protein 26g
Carbohydrate 19g
Sugars 10g
Fat 27g
Saturates 6.5g

INGREDIENTS

175 g/6 oz broccoli

85 g/3 oz asparagus spears, diagonally sliced

1 tbsp virgin olive oil

1 onion, cut into small wedges

2–4 garlic cloves, finely chopped

1 large orange pepper, deseeded and chopped

4 eggs

3 tbsp cold water

25 g/1 oz sesame seeds

15 g/½ oz freshly grated Parmesan cheese

3 spring onions, finely sliced

salt and pepper

1 Break the broccoli into florets, then cook in a saucepan of salted boiling water for 4 minutes. Add the asparagus after 2 minutes. Drain, then plunge into cold water. Drain and reserve.

2 Meanwhile, heat the olive oil in a large frying pan over a low heat, add the onion, garlic and orange pepper and cook, stirring, for 8 minutes, or until the vegetables have softened.

3 Beat the eggs with the water and salt and pepper to taste in a medium-sized bowl. Pour into the frying pan, add the broccoli and asparagus and stir gently. Cook over a medium heat for 3–4 minutes, drawing the mixture from the edges of the pan into the centre, allowing the uncooked egg to flow to the edges of the pan. Preheat the grill.

4 Sprinkle the top of the frittata with the sesame seeds and cheese and cook under the hot grill for 3–5 minutes, or until golden and set. Sprinkle with the spring onions, cut into wedges and serve. Serve either warm or cold.

30 MINUTES TO COOK

Indian-style Omelette

Omelettes are very versatile: they go with almost anything and you can also serve them at any time of the day.

Nutritional Information

Calories 132
Protein 7g
Carbohydrate 2g
Sugars 1g
Fat 11g
Saturates 2g

INGREDIENTS

1 small onion, very finely chopped

2 fresh green chillies, deseeded and finely chopped

2 tbsp finely chopped fresh coriander leaves, plus extra sprigs to garnish

4 eggs

1 tsp salt

2 tbsp vegetable oil

TO SERVE

crisp green salad

mango chutney

1 Place the onion, chillies and coriander in a bowl and mix together.

2 Whisk the eggs in a separate bowl. Stir the onion mixture into the eggs. Add the salt and whisk again.

3 Heat 1 tablespoon of the vegetable oil in a large, heavy-based frying pan over a medium heat. Place a ladleful of the omelette batter in the pan. Cook the omelette, turning once and pressing down with a flat spoon to make sure that the egg is cooked right through, until the omelette is just firm and golden brown.

4 Repeat the same process with the remaining oil and batter. Set the omelettes aside as you make them, and keep warm in a low oven while you make the remaining batches.

5 Serve the omelettes hot, garnished with coriander sprigs and accompanied by a crisp green salad and mango chutney.

COOK'S TIP
Whether intensively farmed or free-range, eggs are susceptible to bacteria. Never use cracked eggs, and store them in the refrigerator for up to 2 weeks, pointed end downwards. Bring them to room temperature about 30 minutes before using.

Thai Fish Cakes

30 MINUTES TO COOK

These little fish cakes are very popular as street food in Thailand and also make a perfect starter with a spicy peanut dip.

Nutritional Information
Calories 205
Protein 17g
Carbohydrate 7g
Sugars 6g
Fat 12g
Saturates 2g

INGREDIENTS

350 g/12 oz white fish fillet, such as cod or haddock, skinned

1 tbsp Thai fish sauce

2 tsp Thai red curry paste

1 tbsp lime juice

1 garlic clove, crushed

4 dried kaffir lime leaves, crumbled

1 egg white

3 tbsp chopped fresh coriander

vegetable oil, for frying

green salad leaves, to serve

PEANUT DIP

1 small fresh red chilli

1 tbsp light soy sauce

1 tbsp lime juice

1 tbsp soft light brown sugar

3 tbsp crunchy peanut butter

4 tbsp coconut milk

salt and pepper

snipped fresh chives, to garnish

1 Place the fish fillet in a food processor with the fish sauce, curry paste, lime juice, garlic, lime leaves and egg white, and process until a smooth paste forms.

2 Add the chopped coriander and quickly process again until mixed. Divide the mixture into 8–10 pieces and roll into balls between the palms of your hands, then flatten to make small round patties and reserve.

3 To make the dip, halve and deseed the chilli, then chop finely. Place in a small saucepan with the soy sauce, lime juice, sugar, peanut butter and coconut milk and heat gently, stirring constantly, until thoroughly blended. Adjust the seasoning, adding more lime juice or sugar to taste.

4 Heat the vegetable oil in a frying pan and fry the fish cakes in batches for 3–4 minutes on each side until golden brown. Drain on kitchen paper and serve hot on a bed of salad leaves with the peanut dip garnished with chives.

30 MINUTES TO COOK

Butterflied Poussins

*The perfect alternative to roast
chicken when you find yourself short
of time or just fancy a change, these
little birds are simply split open and
grilled until tender.*

Nutritional Information

Calories 470
Protein 39g
Carbohydrate 0g
Sugars 0g
Fat 35g
Saturates 15g

INGREDIENTS

4 poussins
55 g/2 oz butter
1 tbsp lemon juice
**1 tbsp chopped fresh parsley,
    plus extra to garnish**
1 tsp chopped fresh tarragon
salt and pepper
mixed salad leaves, to serve

1 Preheat the grill to high. If the
poussins are trussed, remove and
discard the string. Using poultry shears
or kitchen scissors, cut along either
side of the backbone of each bird and
remove. Lay the poussins down and
flatten gently with a rolling pin or the
heel of your hand. Thread a long
skewer from wing to wing and from
leg to leg through each bird to
keep them flat.

2 Melt the butter, brush it over the
poussins and reserve the remainder.
Place the poussins on a grill rack, skin
side uppermost. Sprinkle with lemon
juice, parsley and tarragon and season
to taste with salt and pepper.

3 Cook under the hot grill for
6 minutes, or until golden. Turn them
over, brush with the remaining melted
butter and grill for a further 6 minutes,
or until cooked through. Remove the
skewers and transfer to warmed
serving plates. Garnish with extra
parsley and serve immediately with
mixed salad leaves.

COOK'S TIP

You can thread
the skewers
crossways through
the poussins, if you
like. Push a skewer
through a wing and
out through the
thigh on the
opposite side.
Repeat with the
other skewer on the
other side.

144

Chicken with Pak Choi

Chicken is a source of complete protein, which, like all meats, means it provides all the amino acids that help us to build body structures like skin, bones and teeth. It has less saturated fat than red meat.

Nutritional Information

Calories 233
Protein 31g
Carbohydrate 14g
Sugars 4.8g
Fat 6.6g
Saturates 2.2g

INGREDIENTS

175 g/6 oz broccoli

1 tbsp groundnut oil

2.5-cm/1-inch piece fresh root ginger, finely grated

1 fresh red bird's eye chilli, deseeded and chopped

2 garlic cloves, crushed

1 red onion

450 g/1 lb skinless, boneless chicken breast, cut into thin strips

175 g/6 oz pak choi, shredded

115 g/4 oz baby corn cobs, halved

1 tbsp light soy sauce

1 tbsp Thai fish sauce

1 tbsp chopped fresh coriander

1 tbsp toasted sesame seeds

1 Break the broccoli into small florets and cook in a saucepan of lightly salted boiling water for 3 minutes. Drain and reserve until required.

2 Heat a wok over a high heat until almost smoking, add the groundnut oil and then add the ginger, chilli and garlic. Stir-fry for 1 minute. Cut the onion into wedges and add to the wok with the chicken. Stir-fry for a further 3–4 minutes, or until the chicken is sealed on all sides.

3 Add the remaining vegetables, including the broccoli, and stir-fry for 3–4 minutes, or until tender.

4 Add the soy and Thai fish sauces and stir-fry for a further 1–2 minutes, then serve immediately, sprinkled with the chopped coriander and sesame seeds.

2

30 MINUTES TO COOK

Pan-fried Chicken & Coriander

It is difficult to believe that the rich-tasting sauce coating this flavoursome chicken doesn't contain lashings of double cream. Nevertheless, this is a low-fat dish and all it needs as an accompaniment is a steamed green vegetable or a crisp salad.

Nutritional Information

Calories 200
Protein 27g
Carbohydrate 6g
Sugars 3g
Fat 8g
Saturates 3g

INGREDIENTS

1 bunch of fresh coriander

1 tbsp sunflower or corn oil

4 skinless, boneless chicken breasts, about 115 g/4 oz each, trimmed of all visible fat

1 tsp cornflour

1 tbsp water

90 ml/3 fl oz low-fat natural yogurt

2 tbsp reduced-fat single cream

175 ml/6 fl oz chicken stock

2 tbsp lime juice

2 garlic cloves, finely chopped

1 shallot, finely chopped

1 tomato, peeled, deseeded and chopped

salt and pepper

1 Reserve a few coriander sprigs for a garnish and roughly chop the remainder. Heat the sunflower oil in a heavy-based frying pan, add the chicken and cook over a medium heat for 5 minutes on each side, or until the juices run clear when the meat is pierced with a skewer or the point of a knife. Remove from the frying pan and keep warm.

2 Mix the cornflour and water together until smooth. Stir in the yogurt and cream. Pour the chicken stock and lime juice into the frying pan and add the garlic and shallot. Reduce the heat and simmer for 1 minute. Stir the tomato into the yogurt mixture and stir the mixture into the frying pan. Season to taste with salt and pepper. Cook, stirring constantly, for 1–2 minutes, or until slightly thickened, but do not let the mixture boil. Stir in the chopped fresh coriander.

3 Place the chicken on a large serving plate, pour the sauce over it and garnish with the reserved coriander sprigs. Serve immediately.

COOK'S TIP
Wrap the chicken portions in pieces of foil to keep warm and to prevent them drying out after cooking. Before serving, remove from the foil and transfer to individual serving plates.

148

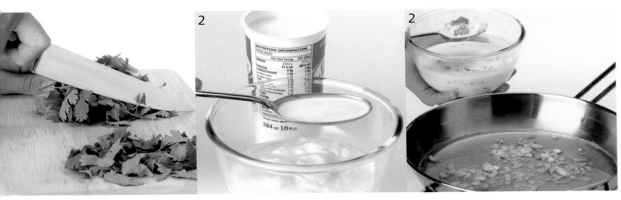

Turkey Breasts with Orange Sauce

30 MINUTES TO COOK

This is a fragrant, summery dish that needs nothing more than a crisp salad to make a light supper.

Nutritional Information
Calories 300
Protein 34g
Carbohydrate 1g
Sugars 1g
Fat 18g
Saturates 9g

INGREDIENTS

4 turkey breast steaks, about 140 g/5 oz each

55 g/2 oz butter

2 tbsp olive oil

6 tbsp chicken stock

3–4 tbsp orange juice

1 tbsp chopped fresh chervil

salt and pepper

TO GARNISH

orange slices

fresh chervil sprigs

1 Place each turkey breast steak in turn between 2 sheets of clingfilm and beat with the side of a rolling pin or the flat surface of a meat mallet until 5 mm/ ¼ inch thick. Season to taste with salt and pepper.

2 Melt half the butter with the olive oil in a large griddle pan. Add half the turkey steaks and cook over a high heat, turning once, for 3–4 minutes, or until lightly browned on both sides. Remove from the griddle pan, add the remaining turkey steaks and cook in the same way. Keep warm.

3 Pour the chicken stock into the griddle pan and bring to the boil, stirring and scraping up any sediment from the base of the griddle pan. Add 3 tablespoons of the orange juice, the remaining butter and the chervil, then reduce the heat to a simmer.

4 Return all the turkey steaks, with any meat juices, to the griddle pan. Simmer gently for 1 minute on each side. Taste and adjust the seasoning, adding more orange juice if necessary. Serve immediately, garnished with orange slices and chervil sprigs.

COOK'S TIP
Blood oranges are a good choice for this dish, as they are very juicy and have a sharp edge to their flavour. If you cannot find blood oranges, use ordinary ones instead.

Chicken Braised in Red Wine

30 MINUTES TO COOK

Rich in colour and flavour, this dish needs little in the way of accompaniments except a little green salad and a glass of the same red wine that is used in the dish.

Nutritional Information
Calories 423
Protein 41g
Carbohydrate 8g
Sugars 7g
Fat 20g
Saturates 5g

INGREDIENTS

3 tbsp olive oil

4 skinless, boneless chicken breasts, about 140 g/5 oz each

1 red onion, halved and sliced

2 tbsp red pesto

300 ml/10 fl oz full-bodied red wine

300 ml/10 fl oz chicken stock or water

115 g/4 oz seedless red grapes, halved

salt and pepper

1 Heat 2 tablespoons of the olive oil in a large, heavy-based frying pan or flameproof casserole. Add the chicken and cook over a medium heat for 3 minutes on each side, or until golden. Remove from the frying pan and reserve until required.

2 Add the remaining olive oil to the frying pan. When it is hot, add the onion and pesto and cook over a low heat, stirring occasionally, for 5 minutes, or until the onion is softened. Pour in the wine and chicken stock and bring to the boil, stirring constantly.

3 Return the chicken to the frying pan, season to taste with salt and pepper, cover and simmer for 15 minutes, or until the chicken is tender. Add the grapes and heat through for 1 minute. Transfer to warmed serving dishes and serve immediately.

COOK'S TIP
If time is short, cut the chicken into small strips or cubes, cook over a medium heat in Step 1 until cooked through and omit the simmering time in Step 3. Make sure the chicken is piping hot before serving.

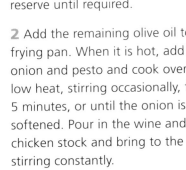

Pork in Creamy Mushroom Sauce

 30 MINUTES TO COOK

The perfect choice for easy entertaining, as the dish looks and tastes fabulous but is actually astonishingly simple to prepare.

Nutritional Information
Calories 424
Protein 40g
Carbohydrate 3g
Sugars 0g
Fat 26g
Saturates 14g

INGREDIENTS

25 g/1 oz unsalted butter

700 g/1 lb 9 oz pork loin, cut into thin strips

280 g/10 oz mixed wild and cultivated
    mushrooms, halved, or quartered
    if large

6 tbsp dry white wine

225 ml/8 fl oz crème fraîche

1 tbsp chopped fresh sage

salt and pepper

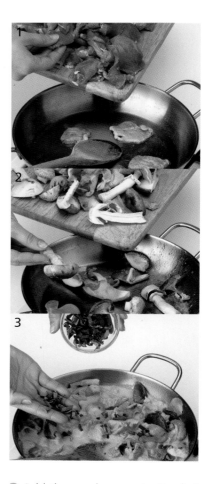

1 Melt the butter in a large, heavy-based frying pan. Add the pork strips and cook over a medium–low heat, stirring frequently, for 5 minutes, or until browned all over. Transfer to a plate with a slotted spoon, season to taste with salt and pepper, cover and keep warm.

2 Add the mushrooms to the frying pan and cook, stirring frequently, for 5–7 minutes, or until tender. Add the wine, bring to the boil and cook until reduced. Add the crème fraîche and return to the boil.

3 Return the pork to the frying pan, stir in the sage and heat through for 1–2 minutes. Transfer to a warmed serving dish and serve immediately.

COOK'S TIP
If possible, try to use fresh herbs, which have a much better flavour than dried. If they are not available, use freeze-dried herbs instead. These are found in most large supermarkets.

30 MINUTES TO COOK   Thai-spiced Sausages

*These mildly spiced little sausages
are a good choice for a buffet meal.
They are equally good hot or cold.*

Nutritional Information
Calories 206
Protein 22g
Carbohydrate 4g
Sugars 0g
Fat 11g
Saturates 2g

INGREDIENTS

400 g/14 oz fresh lean pork mince

4 tbsp cooked rice

1 garlic clove, crushed

1 tsp Thai red curry paste

1 tsp pepper

1 tsp ground coriander

½ tsp salt

3 tbsp lime juice

2 tbsp chopped fresh coriander

3 tbsp groundnut oil

cucumber and fresh chilli spirals, to garnish

mixed salad leaves, to serve

1 Place the pork, rice, garlic, curry
paste, pepper, ground coriander, salt,
lime juice and chopped coriander in a
bowl and knead together with your
hands to mix evenly.

2 Use your hands to shape the mixture
into 12 small sausage shapes. If you
can buy sausage casings, fill the casings
and twist at intervals.

3 Heat the groundnut oil in a large
frying pan over a medium heat. Add
the sausages, in batches if necessary,
and fry for 8–10 minutes, turning them
over occasionally, until they are evenly
golden brown. Garnish with cucumber
and chilli spirals and serve with salad.

COOK'S TIP
These sausages can also be served as a
starter – shape the mixture into slightly
smaller shapes to make about
16 bite-sized sausages. Serve them with
a soy dip.

15 mins

 15 mins

serves 4

30 MINUTES TO COOK Beef Kebabs

This simple dish tastes wonderful and would make a delicious treat for any occasion. It would also be ideal for a barbecue party.

Nutritional Information
Calories 335
Protein 40g
Carbohydrate 2g
Sugars 2g
Fat 19g
Saturates 4g

INGREDIENTS

8 spring onions

700 g/1 lb 9 oz rump steak, cut into cubes

8 cherry tomatoes, halved

1 tbsp wholegrain mustard

1 tsp Worcestershire sauce

½ tsp balsamic vinegar

4 tbsp sunflower oil

salt and pepper

1 Preheat the grill to medium. Cut the spring onions into 10–13-cm/4–5-inch lengths and halve lengthways. Thread the steak cubes, spring onion lengths and cherry tomato halves alternately onto 4 metal or presoaked wooden skewers. Arrange them on a grill rack.

2 Mix the mustard, Worcestershire sauce and vinegar together in a small bowl. Whisk in the sunflower oil and season to taste with salt and pepper.

3 Brush the kebabs with the flavoured oil and cook under the hot grill for 4 minutes. Turn over, brush with the flavoured oil again and cook for 4 minutes. Transfer to a large serving plate and serve immediately.

COOK'S TIP
It is quicker to use metal skewers, as wooden ones need to be soaked in warm water for 30 minutes before using to prevent them burning while cooking. If using metal ones, use oven gloves to pick them up as they will be hot.

30 MINUTES TO COOK   Beef with Eggs

This delicacy comes from Thailand, although similar recipes exist in the cuisines of other Asian countries. Only one saucepan is used, although the dish is cooked in individual ramekins.

Nutritional Information
Calories 124
Protein 12g
Carbohydrate 1g
Sugars 0g
Fat 8g
Saturates 2g

INGREDIENTS

115 g/4 oz sirloin steak, finely chopped
1 tsp grated fresh root ginger
1 tbsp Thai fish sauce
3 eggs
125 ml/4 fl oz chicken stock
3 spring onions, finely chopped
pepper
4 whole spring onions, to garnish

1 Mix the steak, ginger and fish sauce together in a bowl and season to taste with pepper.

2 Beat the eggs with the chicken stock in a separate bowl. Stir the egg mixture into the steak mixture and add the spring onions. Whisk until blended.

3 Set a steamer over a saucepan of gently simmering water. Pour the steak and egg mixture into 4 ramekins and place them in the steamer. Cover and steam for 10–15 minutes, or until set. Remove from the steamer and leave to cool slightly before serving. Garnish with the whole spring onions.

COOK'S TIP
If you are going to serve this dish as a starter, this quantity is enough for 6 people. If you don't have time to make a stock, use water instead.

160

30 MINUTES TO COOK   **Meatballs on Sticks**

These are popular with children and adults alike. Serve with a selection of ready-made or home-made sauces, such as a tomato relish heated on the side of the barbecue.

Nutritional Information
Calories 132
Protein 9g
Carbohydrate 8g
Sugars 2g
Fat 7g
Saturates 3g

INGREDIENTS

4 pork and herb sausages

115 g/4 oz fresh beef mince

85 g/3 oz fresh white breadcrumbs

1 onion, finely chopped

2 tbsp chopped mixed fresh herbs, such as parsley, thyme and sage

1 egg

sunflower oil, for brushing

salt and pepper

sauces of your choice, to serve

1 Preheat the barbecue. Remove the sausage meat from the skins, place in a large bowl and break up with a fork. Add the beef mince, breadcrumbs, onion, mixed herbs and egg. Season to taste with salt and pepper and stir well with a wooden spoon until thoroughly mixed.

2 Form the mixture into small balls, about the size of a golf ball, between the palms of your hands. Spear each one with a wooden cocktail stick and brush with sunflower oil.

3 Cook over medium hot coals, turning frequently and brushing with more oil as necessary, for 10 minutes, or until cooked through. Transfer to a large serving plate and serve immediately with a sauce of your choice.

COOK'S TIP
An increasing number of flavoured sausages are available, from leek and black pepper to chilli, and can be used for these meatballs.

30 MINUTES TO COOK Mexican Prawns

For a very special treat, you could use large or tiger prawns for this tasty dish. If the prawns are frozen, make sure that they are fully thawed out before you begin cooking.

Nutritional Information
Calories 189
Protein 27g
Carbohydrate 9g
Sugars 7g
Fat 7g
Saturates 1g

INGREDIENTS

1 fresh green chilli

1 tbsp sunflower or corn oil

1 large onion, finely chopped

3 garlic cloves, finely chopped

3 beef tomatoes, peeled, deseeded and chopped

1 bay leaf

450 g/1 lb cooked peeled prawns

1 tbsp lime juice

few sprigs of fresh coriander, plus extra to garnish

salt and pepper

COOK'S TIP
It is difficult to estimate how hot chillies are unless you know the variety, and even then, individual specimens may vary. Dark green chillies are usually much hotter than pale green ones.

1 Using a sharp knife, cut the chilli in half and remove and discard the seeds, then chop finely and reserve.

2 Heat the sunflower oil in a large, heavy-based frying pan. Add the onion and garlic and cook over a low heat, stirring occasionally, for 5 minutes, or until softened.

3 Add the chopped tomatoes, chopped chilli and bay leaf and simmer over a low heat, stirring occasionally, for 10 minutes, or until thickened.

4 Toss the prawns in the lime juice and stir into the sauce. Chop the coriander and stir into the sauce. Season to taste with salt and pepper. Cook for a further 4 minutes, or until heated through. Transfer to 4 large serving bowls and garnish with fresh coriander sprigs. Serve immediately.

30 MINUTES TO COOK Thai Prawn Curry

Thai cooking is renowned for its subtle blending of aromatic spices and this mouthwatering curry is no exception.

Nutritional Information

Calories 150
Protein 11g
Carbohydrate 6g
Sugars 4g
Fat 9g
Saturates 1g

INGREDIENTS

450 g/1 lb raw tiger prawns
2 tbsp groundnut oil
2 tbsp Thai green curry paste
4 kaffir lime leaves, shredded
1 lemon grass stalk, chopped
225 ml/8 fl oz coconut milk
2 tbsp Thai fish sauce
½ cucumber, deseeded and cut into batons
12 fresh basil leaves, plus extra to garnish
2 fresh green chillies, sliced

1 Peel and devein the prawns. Heat the groundnut oil in a preheated wok or heavy-based frying pan. Add the curry paste and cook over a medium heat for 1 minute, or until it is bubbling and releases its aroma.

2 Add the prawns, lime leaves and lemon grass and stir-fry for 2 minutes, or until the prawns have turned pink.

3 Stir in the coconut milk and bring to the boil, then reduce the heat and simmer, stirring occasionally, for 5 minutes. Stir in the fish sauce, cucumber and basil. Transfer to a warmed serving dish. Scatter over the chilli slices, garnish with fresh basil leaves and serve.

COOK'S TIP
Three types of basil are used in Thailand: hairy (bai mangluk), sweet (bai horapa) and Thai or holy basil (bai grapao). They are all more strongly flavoured than Western basil.

15 mins

 12 mins

 serves 4

30 MINUTES TO COOK   Haddock in a Cheese Jacket

These fish fillets are smothered not in an ordinary cheese sauce but in a more unusual cheese-flavoured paste, which gives them a lovely golden jacket, making them especially popular with children.

Nutritional Information
Calories 386
Protein 43g
Carbohydrate 7g
Sugars 1g
Fat 21g
Saturates 10g

INGREDIENTS

2 tbsp olive oil, plus extra for brushing
4 haddock fillets, about 175 g/6 oz each
grated rind and juice of 2 lemons
115 g/4 oz Gruyère cheese, grated
4 tbsp fresh white breadcrumbs
4 tbsp crème fraîche
4 garlic cloves, finely chopped
salt and pepper
TO GARNISH
lemon wedges
fresh parsley sprigs

1 Preheat the oven to 200°C/400°F/ Gas Mark 6. Brush a roasting tin or large ovenproof dish with olive oil and arrange the fish in it in a single layer. Sprinkle with a little lemon juice and season to taste with salt and pepper.

2 Mix the olive oil, cheese, breadcrumbs, crème fraîche, garlic, lemon rind and 6 tablespoons of the remaining lemon juice together in a large bowl and season to taste with salt and pepper. Spread the cheese paste evenly over the fish fillets.

3 Bake in the preheated oven for 12–15 minutes, or until the fish is cooked through. Transfer to warmed serving plates, garnish with lemon wedges and parsley sprigs and serve.

COOK'S TIP
It is quite easy to overcook fish. When the fish is done, the flesh should be opaque nearly all the way through and it should flake easily when tested with a fork.

30 MINUTES TO COOK   Finnan Haddie

Finnan haddock is, in fact, a small whole haddock that has been soaked in brine before cold smoking. However, you can use undyed smoked haddock fillet for this traditional Scottish dish.

Nutritional Information
Calories 320
Protein 33g
Carbohydrate 4g
Sugars 4g
Fat 19g
Saturates 10g

INGREDIENTS

500 g/1 lb 2 oz smoked haddock, skinned and cut into chunks

225 ml/8 fl oz milk

125 ml/4 fl oz single cream

25 g/1 oz unsalted butter

4 eggs

pepper

1 Preheat the oven to 180°C/350°F/Gas Mark 4. Place the chunks of fish in a large ovenproof dish. Pour the milk and cream into a small saucepan, add the butter, season to taste with pepper and heat gently until the butter has melted. Pour the mixture over the fish.

2 Bake in the preheated oven for 20 minutes, or until the fish is tender.

3 Meanwhile, bring a small saucepan of water to the boil. Break an egg into a cup, stir the water to create a small 'whirlpool' and slide in the egg. Poach for 3–4 minutes, or until the white is set but the yolk is still soft. Remove and drain, trimming any stray strings of white, if necessary. Poach the remaining eggs in the same way. Top the fish with the eggs and serve.

COOK'S TIP
Look for undyed, smoked haddock, which is a more attractive colour, has a better flavour and is healthier. It is usually available from most supermarkets.

30 MINUTES TO COOK

Mackerel with Lime

The secret of this dish lies in the simple, fresh flavours, which perfectly complement the richness of the barbecued fish.

Nutritional Information
Calories 302
Protein 21g
Carbohydrate 0g
Sugars 0g
Fat 24g
Saturates 4g

INGREDIENTS

4 small mackerel

¼ tsp ground coriander

¼ tsp ground cumin

4 fresh coriander sprigs

3 tbsp chopped fresh coriander

1 fresh red chilli, deseeded and chopped

grated rind and juice of 1 lime

2 tbsp sunflower oil

salt and pepper

TO GARNISH

1 lime, sliced

fresh chilli flowers (optional)

salad leaves, to serve

1 Preheat the barbecue. To make chilli flowers, cut the tip of small chillies lengthways into thin strips, leaving the chillies intact at the stem end. Remove the seeds and place in iced water.

2 Clean and gut the mackerel, if this has not been done by the fishmonger, removing the heads if preferred. Rinse and pat dry. Sprinkle the fish with the ground spices and salt and pepper to taste. Sprinkle 1 teaspoon of chopped coriander inside the cavity of each fish.

3 Mix the chopped coriander, chilli, lime rind and juice and the sunflower oil together in a small bowl. Brush the mixture liberally over the fish.

4 Place the fish in a hinged rack. Barbecue over hot coals for 3–4 minutes on each side, turning once. Brush frequently with the remaining basting mixture. Transfer to plates and garnish with chilli flowers, if using, and lime slices, and serve with salad leaves.

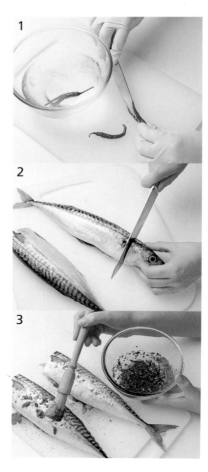

COOK'S TIP
This recipe is suitable for other oily fish, such as trout, herring or sardines.

172

30 MINUTES TO COOK   Spinach & Herb Frittata

If you find the prospect of turning over a Spanish tortilla daunting, try this Italian version of a flat omelette, which finishes cooking under a grill.

Nutritional Information
Calories 145
Protein 8g
Carbohydrate 1g
Sugars 0g
Fat 12g
Saturates 13g

INGREDIENTS

4 tbsp olive oil

6 spring onions, sliced

250 g/9 oz young spinach leaves, any coarse stems removed, rinsed

6 large eggs

3 tbsp finely chopped mixed fresh herbs, such as flat-leaf parsley, thyme and coriander

2 tbsp freshly grated Parmesan cheese, plus extra for garnishing

salt and pepper

fresh flat-leaf parsley sprigs, to garnish

mixed salad leaves, to serve

1 Heat a 2-cm/10-inch non-stick frying pan with a flameproof handle. Add the oil and heat. Add the spring onions and cook for 2 minutes.

2 Add the spinach and cook until it just wilts.

3 Beat the eggs in a large bowl and season to taste with salt and pepper. Using a slotted spoon, transfer the spinach and onions to the bowl of eggs and stir in the herbs. Pour the excess oil left in the frying pan into a heatproof jug, then scrape off the crusty bits from the base of the pan.

4 Reheat the pan. Add 2 tablespoons of the reserved oil. Pour in the egg mixture, smoothing it into an even layer. Cook, shaking the pan occasionally, for 6 minutes, or until the base is set when you lift up the side with a spatula. Preheat the grill.

5 Sprinkle the top of the frittata with the Parmesan cheese, then place under the hot grill and cook for 3 minutes, or until the excess liquid is set and the cheese is golden.

6 Remove from the heat and slide the frittata onto a serving plate. Leave for at least 5 minutes before cutting and garnishing with extra Parmesan and parsley. Serve with a mixed salad.

15 mins

15 mins

serves 6

30 MINUTES TO COOK   Roasted Vegetables

If you have time, rosemary branches can be used as skewers. Soak the rosemary skewers overnight to prevent them charring.

Nutritional Information

Calories 16
Protein 1g
Carbohydrate 3g
Sugars 3g
Fat 0.3g
Saturates 0g

INGREDIENTS

1 small red cabbage

1 fennel bulb

1 orange pepper, cut into 4-cm/1½-inch dice

1 aubergine, halved and sliced into 1-cm/½-inch pieces

2 courgettes, diagonally thickly sliced

6 rosemary twigs, about 15 cm/6 inches long, soaked in cold water

olive oil, for brushing

salt and pepper

1 Preheat the barbecue or grill. Place the red cabbage on its side on a chopping board and cut through the middle of its stem and heart. Divide each piece into 4, each time including a section of the stem in the slice to hold it together.

2 Prepare the fennel in the same way as the red cabbage.

3 Blanch the red cabbage and fennel in boiling water for 3 minutes, then drain well.

4 With a wooden skewer, carefully pierce a hole through the middle of each piece of vegetable.

5 Thread a piece of orange pepper, fennel, red cabbage, aubergine and courgette onto each rosemary twig, gently pushing the rosemary through the skewer holes.

6 Brush liberally with olive oil and season with plenty of salt and pepper.

7 Cook over medium hot coals or under the hot grill for 8–10 minutes, turning occasionally. Serve immediately.

VARIATION
Fruit skewers are a deliciously quick and easy dessert. Thread pieces of banana, mango, peach, strawberry, apple and pear onto skewers and cook over the dying embers. Brush with sugar syrup towards the end of cooking.

176

5   6

Filo Tartlets with Avocado Salsa

30 MINUTES TO COOK

Filo pastry makes crisp little containers for a spicy avocado salsa. If you are making these for a party, fill them just before serving.

Nutritional Information
Calories 49
Protein 1g
Carbohydrate 3g
Sugars 1g
Fat 4g
Saturates 2g

INGREDIENTS

TARTLET CASES
70 g/2½ oz ready-made filo pastry
3 tbsp melted butter, plus extra for greasing
AVOCADO SALSA
1 large avocado
1 small red onion, finely chopped
1 fresh chilli, deseeded and finely chopped
2 tomatoes, peeled, deseeded and finely chopped
juice of 1 lime
2 tbsp chopped fresh coriander
salt and pepper

1 Preheat the oven to 180°C/350°F/ Gas Mark 4. To make the tartlet cases, working with 1 sheet of filo pastry at a time and keeping the rest covered with a cloth, brush the pastry sheet with melted butter. With a sharp knife, cut the sheet into 5-cm/2-inch squares.

2 Grease 20 cups in mini muffin trays and line each one with 3 buttered filo pastry squares, setting each one at an angle to the others. Repeat until all the pastry is used up. Bake in the oven for 6–8 minutes, or until crisp and golden. Carefully transfer to a wire rack to cool.

3 To make the salsa, peel the avocado and remove the stone. Cut the flesh into small dice, place in a bowl with the onion, chilli, tomatoes, lime juice and coriander, and add salt and pepper to taste. Divide the salsa between the pastry cases and serve immediately.

COOK'S TIP
The pastry cases can be made up to a week in advance and stored in an airtight container. Make the salsa just before serving. Once the cases are filled, serve them straight away, otherwise they will go soft.

Instant Pesto & Goat's Cheese Tartlets

30 MINUTES TO COOK

The puff pastry in these tartlets rises up around the flavoursome filling to make an instant pastry case!

Nutritional Information
Calories 66
Protein 2g
Carbohydrate 4g
Sugars 1g
Fat 5g
Saturates 1g

INGREDIENTS

plain flour, for dusting

200 g/7 oz ready-made puff pastry

3 tbsp pesto

20 cherry tomatoes, each cut into 3 slices

115 g/4 oz goat's cheese

salt and pepper

fresh basil sprigs, to garnish

1 Preheat the oven to 200°C/400°F/ Gas Mark 6, then lightly flour a baking sheet. Roll out the pastry on a floured work surface to 3 mm/⅛ inch thick. Cut out 20 rounds with a 5-cm/2-inch plain cutter and arrange the pastry rounds on the floured baking sheet.

2 Spread a little pesto on each round, leaving a margin around the edges, then arrange 3 tomato slices on top of each one.

3 Crumble the goat's cheese over and season with salt and pepper. Bake in the oven for 10 minutes, or until the pastry is puffed up, crisp and golden. Garnish with basil and serve warm.

COOK'S TIP
These tartlets are even quicker to make if you use the ready-rolled variety of ready-made puff pastry, which is available in most large supermarkets.

Tofu & Vegetable Stir-fry

10 mins

20 mins

serves 4

This is a quick dish to prepare, making it the perfect choice for a midweek supper dish, after a busy day at work!

Nutritional Information

Calories 124
Protein 6g
Carbohydrate 11g
Sugars 2g
Fat 6g
Saturates 1g

INGREDIENTS

175 g/6 oz potatoes, cubed

1 tbsp vegetable oil

1 red onion, sliced

225 g/8 oz firm tofu (drained weight), diced

2 courgettes, diced

8 canned artichoke hearts, halved

150 ml/5 fl oz passata

1 tbsp sweet chilli sauce

1 tbsp soy sauce

1 tsp caster sugar

2 tbsp chopped fresh basil

salt and pepper

1 Cook the potatoes in a saucepan of lightly salted boiling water for 10 minutes. Drain thoroughly and reserve until required.

2 Heat the vegetable oil in a preheated wok or large frying pan and stir-fry the red onion for 2 minutes, or until it has softened.

3 Stir in the tofu and courgettes and stir-fry for 3–4 minutes, or until they begin to brown slightly.

4 Add the cooked potatoes to the wok, stirring gently to mix.

5 Stir in the artichoke hearts, passata, sweet chilli sauce, soy sauce, sugar and chopped basil.

6 Season to taste with salt and pepper and cook for a further 5 minutes, stirring constantly.

7 Transfer the tofu and vegetable stir-fry to individual serving dishes and serve immediately.

COOK'S TIP
Canned artichoke hearts should be drained thoroughly and rinsed well before use because they often have salt added.

15 mins

 15 mins

serves 4

Chargrilled Vegetables

This medley of peppers, courgettes, aubergine and red onion can be served on its own or as an unusual side dish.

Nutritional Information

Calories 66

Protein 7g

Carbohydrate 7g

Sugars 7g

Fat 3g

Saturates 0.5g

INGREDIENTS

1 large red pepper

1 large green pepper

1 large orange pepper

1 large courgette

4 baby aubergines

2 red onions

2 tbsp lemon juice

1 tbsp olive oil

1 garlic clove, crushed

1 tbsp chopped fresh rosemary or 1 tsp dried rosemary

salt and pepper

TO SERVE

freshly cooked bulgar wheat

tomato and olive relish

1 Preheat the grill or barbecue. Halve and deseed the peppers and cut into even-sized pieces, 2.5 cm/1 inch wide.

2 Trim the courgettes, cut in half lengthways and slice into 2.5-cm/1-inch pieces. Place the peppers and courgettes in a large bowl.

3 Trim the aubergines and quarter them lengthways. Peel the onions, then cut each of them into 8 even-sized wedges. Add the aubergines and onions to the peppers and courgettes.

4 Whisk the lemon juice, olive oil, garlic and rosemary together in a small bowl. Season to taste with salt and pepper. Pour the mixture over the vegetables and stir to coat evenly.

5 Thread the vegetables onto 8 metal or presoaked wooden skewers. Arrange the kebabs on the grill rack and cook under the hot grill, turning frequently, for 10–12 minutes, or until the vegetables are lightly charred and just softened. Alternatively, cook over hot coals, turning frequently, for 8–10 minutes, or until softened and beginning to char.

6 Drain the kebabs and serve immediately on a bed of bulgar wheat with a tomato and olive relish.

10 mins

 15 mins

 serves 4

Masala Okra

30 MINUTES TO COOK

Also known as bhindi, gumbo and ladies' fingers, okra are small, five-sided, tapering pods that are very popular in the cuisines of India, the Caribbean and the southern United States. This is a spicy Indian dish that would go well with any type of curry. It is suitable for both vegetarians and vegans.

Nutritional Information

Calories 134
Protein 4g
Carbohydrate 5g
Sugars 4g
Fat 11g
Saturates 3g

INGREDIENTS

1 tbsp ground coriander
1 tbsp ground cumin
1 tsp chilli powder
½ tsp ground turmeric
1 tbsp desiccated coconut
pinch of sugar
1 tbsp lime juice
2 tbsp chopped fresh coriander
pinch of salt
3 tbsp groundnut oil
½ tsp black mustard seeds
½ tsp cumin seeds
450 g/1 lb okra
chopped tomato, to garnish

1 Mix the ground coriander, ground cumin, chilli powder, turmeric, coconut, sugar, lime juice, fresh coriander and salt together in a bowl.

2 Heat the groundnut oil in a heavy-based frying pan or preheated wok. Add the mustard seeds and cumin seeds and cook, stirring constantly, for 2 minutes, or until the seeds begin to release their aroma and pop. Stir in the coconut mixture and cook, stirring constantly, for 2 minutes.

3 Add the okra and stir to mix with the spices. Cover and cook for 10 minutes, or until tender. Transfer to a warmed serving dish, garnish with chopped tomato and serve.

COOK'S TIP
Preparing okra for cooking is very simple. Wash it in cold water and pat dry with kitchen paper, then trim the ends with a sharp knife, if you like.

5 mins

 25 mins

serves 6

30 MINUTES TO COOK   Lemon Soufflé

A hot soufflé makes a spectacular end to a meal and this delicious, lemon-flavoured confection is the perfect palate cleanser. All hot soufflés will collapse disappointingly if left to stand, so make sure that you serve it as soon as it is ready.

Nutritional Information

Calories 177
Protein 7g
Carbohydrate 15g
Sugars 12g
Fat 10g
Saturates 5g

INGREDIENTS

25 g/1 oz unsalted butter, plus extra for greasing
25 g/1 oz icing sugar
300 ml/10 fl oz milk
25 g/1 oz plain flour
grated rind and juice of 1 lemon
5 egg yolks
2 tbsp caster sugar
6 egg whites

1 Preheat the oven to 180°C/350°F/ Gas Mark 4. Grease a 1.4-litre/2½-pint soufflé dish with butter and dust the base and sides with icing sugar. Pour the milk into a small saucepan and bring to simmering point.

2 Meanwhile, melt the butter in a heavy-based saucepan over a low heat. Remove from the heat and stir in the flour until a smooth paste forms. Gradually stir in the hot milk. Return to the heat and cook, stirring, for 2 minutes, or until thickened and smooth. Stir in the lemon rind and juice and reserve.

3 Beat the egg yolks with the caster sugar until pale, then gradually stir them into the lemon mixture, adding only a little at a time.

4 Whisk the egg whites in a spotlessly clean, greasefree bowl until stiff peaks form. Fold the egg whites into the lemon mixture. Spoon into the dish and bake in the preheated oven for 20 minutes, or until risen and golden brown. Serve.

COOK'S TIP
If you are planning to serve this delicious dessert to guests at a dinner party, you can prepare the soufflé up to the end of Step 2 in advance.

30 MINUTES TO COOK

Totally Tropical Pineapple

The delicious sweet aroma of fresh pineapple and rum as this succulent, mouthwatering dessert is cooking will transport you to a Caribbean beach. The ground ginger adds just a touch of spice.

Nutritional Information
Calories 206
Protein 1g
Carbohydrate 20g
Sugars 20g
Fat 12g
Saturates 7g

INGREDIENTS

1 pineapple

3 tbsp dark rum

2 tbsp muscovado sugar

1 tsp ground root ginger

4 tbsp unsalted butter, melted

1 Preheat the barbecue. Using a sharp knife, cut off the crown of the pineapple, then cut the fruit into 2-cm/¾-inch thick slices. Cut away the skin from each slice and flick out the 'eyes' with the point of the knife. Stamp out the cores with an apple corer or small pastry cutter.

2 Mix the rum, sugar, ginger and butter together in a jug, stirring constantly, until the sugar has dissolved. Brush the pineapple rings with the rum mixture.

3 Cook the pineapple rings over hot coals for 3–4 minutes on each side. Transfer to serving plates and serve immediately with the remaining rum mixture poured over them.

COOK'S TIP
If possible, use a separate grill rack or barbecue to cook the pineapple on. It is best to use a pair of long-handled tongs to turn the pineapple rings over while they are cooking.

Index